Into the
Garden

Torn Curtain Publishing
Wellington, New Zealand
www.torncurtainpublishing.com

© Copyright 2021 Michelle Zombos. All rights reserved.

ISBN Softcover 978-0-646-99941-8

The events, conversations and locations mentioned in this book represent the author's best memory of them. In order to maintain their anonymity, in some instances the author may have changed the names of individuals and places. This book is not intended as a substitute for professional counselling or medical advice.

No portion of this book may be reproduced, stored in a retrieval system or transmitted in any form or by any means—electronic, mechanical, photocopy, recording or otherwise—except for brief quotations in printed reviews of promotion, without prior written permission from the author.

Unless otherwise noted, all scripture is taken from the Holy Bible, New International Version®, NIV®. Copyright © 1973, 1978, 1984, 2011 by Biblica, Inc.™ Used by permission of Zondervan. All rights reserved worldwide.

Scripture quotations marked NLT are taken from the Holy Bible, New Living Translation, copyright © 1996, 2004, 2015 by Tyndale House Foundation. Used by permission of Tyndale House Publishers, Inc., Carol Stream, Illinois 60188. All rights reserved.

Scripture quotations marked ESV are taken from the Holy Bible, English Standard Version, copyright © 2001 by Crossway, a publishing ministry of Good News Publishers. Used by permission. All rights reserved.

All scripture in bold or in parentheses denote the author's emphasis.

Cover image by Unsplash ©2021. Used with permission.

Cataloguing in Publishing Data
  Title: Into the Garden
  Author: Michelle Zombos
  Subjects: Christian living; marriage and family; mental health and wellbeing; spiritual growth; cross-cultural missions; spiritual life

A copy of this title is held at the National Library of Australia.

Into the Garden

AN INVITATION TO HOLISTIC RESTORATION

MICHELLE ZOMBOS

This book is dedicated to Jamal, Kiara, Lydia, Matthias and Wesley. Thank you for patiently waiting as I went on my journey of holistic restoration. I love you from the depths of my heart.

And to my mother who watched over me in my night seasons. You inspired me and cheered me on, and for that, I'm forever thankful.

Contents

Prologue	11
Chapter 1. The Garden: *God's Intention*	15
Chapter 2. The River: *God's Flow*	27
Chapter 3. The Dirt: *God's Place of Rest*	41
Chapter 4. The Weeds: *Restoring Identity*	51
Chapter 5. The Water: *Restoring Soul*	67
Chapter 6. The Sprouting: *Restoring Calling*	81
Chapter 7. The Branches: *Restoring Community*	91
Chapter 8. The Roots: *Restoring Hearts*	105
Chapter 9. The Pruning: *Restoring Relationship*	117
Chapter 10. The Fruit: *Restoring Prosperity*	127
Chapter 11. The Boundaries: *Restoring Freedom*	135
Chapter 12. The Future: *Restoring Hope*	143
Recommended Resources	153
Acknowledgements	155

> *"The land is like the garden of Eden before them, but behind them a desolate wilderness."*
>
> —Joel 2:3, ESV

Prologue

Have you ever had the sense you were created for something more than this? Something more than your current reality? That perhaps what you're experiencing is not how it was meant to be? That somehow you lucked out on your 'best life'—not because you haven't tried to attain it, but because of circumstances that, unbeknownst to you, existed before you were even born?

You feel this way because you were created for *the garden.*

It's there, in the creation narrative. God established a perfect place for us—the Garden of Eden. Intended to be a sanctuary for humanity for all time, this garden was intentionally designed with us, His most beloved creation, in mind. It was a reflection of the Father's heart for His children.

In the garden, we had nothing to worry about. There was room to move, freedom to grow and stretch out—we had the capacity and the impetuous ability to fill the earth. Nakedness was our friend and vulnerability our greatest ally. Our dreams and ideas were not hindered by fear or doubt; rather, creativity was nurtured and natural, as we emulated the example of the One who set us there. Fresh produce grew, perfectly nourishing our bodies. All our supply was there and all of our needs were met. Fear found no landing place, for God Himself walked with us and protected us, and because we were so aware of the Presence of the Almighty, we had no insecurities. We were intricately caught up in only one thing: the affairs of the King. Satisfied by this relationship, we craved nothing more. We had no one to judge because we lacked the knowledge of good and evil. But then the enemy subtly convinced us that we needed to know such things.

> 'You will not certainly die,' the serpent said to the woman. 'For God knows that when you eat from it your eyes will be opened, and you will be like God, knowing good and evil.'
>
> Genesis 3:4-5

Truth be told, Adam and Eve were actually already like God—created in His image, they displayed so much of His nature already. They were whole and complete, wanting nothing. But the enemy emphasised the fact that there *was* something lacking, subtly convincing them that what was forbidden, was because God was withholding something of value from them. Yet God only ever wanted the best for them. Of all that God had created, He had made only one tree off-limits—so they could live in a freedom that would alleviate them from the responsibility to judge and be judged.

Sadly, Adam and Eve chose to believe the lie of the enemy rather than trust the Word of God. Consequently, their world grew smaller—and so, too, did ours. With the fall of mankind—the disobedient act of one man, Adam—we lost all access to the garden (Genesis 3). Separated from the garden with no hope of return, Adam and Eve, as the forerunners of humanity, were destined to spend the remainder of their days wandering, the consequences of this one choice rippling down to every generation. Our hearts, too, yearn to return to the garden. We, the humanity represented in Adam and Eve, feel from deep within this incessant desire for what should have been.

And yet, while all seemed bleak and irreparable, a restoration plan was executed in the throne room of heaven.

> *For if, by the trespass of the one man, death reigned through that one man, how much more will those who receive God's abundant provision of grace and of the gift of righteousness reign in life through the one man, Jesus Christ!*
>
> Romans 5:17

While Adam brought death into the world, Jesus brought life and restoration. In His love for us, God made a way for us to reign again through His Son. In His delight for us, He invited us back into a spacious place—a place where there is freedom and joy. The God who turned us out of the garden gave up His most precious possession to buy our return ticket home, and while the price was unbearably high, it was an investment He knew would produce an invaluable return. He knew it would mean we could once again know the intimacy and security of His presence. Only this time, the garden wouldn't be an external fortress, but an internal and eternal place of rest.

In nature, a garden is represented as an open space that can produce seed bearing plants, flowers, trees, and grasses. This open space is what I once longed for and now know. But for a long time, I felt stuck in a place I was not meant to be. Then one day, when I was looking through the wooden-framed, floor-to-ceiling windows of my lounge, I noticed how all the plants in my 'garden' were confined to a box.

In that moment, God gently dropped in my spirit that those planter boxes were what my home country, New Zealand, represented for me. The view through my window mirrored what I was feeling inside. Seedling trays, planter boxes, and flowerpots limit growth; they can only provide so much space for us to grow. I realised that God wanted to take me out of the planter box of New Zealand and *into the garden* so I could freely grow. God was calling me into a global adventure—into wide open spaces. He was trying to tell me that this was not my lot or my 'plot,' but that outside of my comfort zone and the land into which I was born, I could experience more growth. Little did I know how many flowerpots He would take me out of as He worked in me to bring about holistic restoration. Leaving New Zealand in 2011 was only the first step into a restorative process that would see my life flourish into what it is today.

God has often used the imagery of nature to reach my heart. It is my

'God space'—a term Doug Pollock coined to describe, "a space where God is…encountered in…ways that address the longings and cries of the heart. In God space, the 'unworthy' feel safe enough to bring their real selves…into the light, and to the journey, one step at a time, toward the magnetic pull they sense deep in their souls. It's a space where spiritual curiosity is aroused, and the message of Christianity becomes plausible" *(God Space, pp. 20-21).*

'Nature' has two definitions. It is both "the phenomena of the physical world collectively, including plants, animals, the landscape, and other features and products of the earth, as opposed to humans or human creations," and "the basic or inherent features, character, or qualities of something."

God has inherent features, characteristics, and qualities that He desires us to discover. He expresses His 'nature' through what we see in nature! He also expresses His nature through story. Your story, my story, and the stories we gather from generations past all reveal something of the nature of God as we seek to find Him in the midst of them.

What I've discovered in writing my story, is that He was there all along. Through the confusion and the trauma, He was by my side, empathising and agonising right along with me. In the moments of joy and celebration, He leaped in my spirit to remind me that He is there with me, experiencing the delight I experience. It's all in His nature.

My life is a testimony of how God works through seasons of difficulty and the 'winter cold' to produce in us a beauty and goodness that display His glory. And He wants to do the same for you. He wants you to know when you journey through dark places that there is glory—there is a garden—waiting for you on the other side of the pain.

CHAPTER ONE

The Garden

God's Intention

My friend's lush green backyard in Ethiopia was framed by a beautiful garden that bloomed with frangipanis and hibiscus flowers and palm trees that reminded me of home. A pathway led to a garden hut, where we would sit to talk while the children swam in the pool or played in the treehouse. The weather was always perfect in that part of Ethiopia. The days were hot, but never scorching as they could be in other parts, and as a result, the garden was vibrant with colour, a wonderful oasis amidst the dusty streets of my own neighbourhood.

Do you know that God created you specifically to live not only in an appointed time in history, but also within the boundaries of a certain land? Acts 17:26 tells us: "From one man he made all the nations, that they should inhabit the whole earth; and he marked out their appointed times in history and the boundaries of their lands."

God wanted His beloved children to inhabit the whole earth, and, while mapping out the part I was going to play, He somehow saw that I was fit for a land far from my wildest dreams: Ethiopia. He called this little girl from New Zealand to that great land, and these pages are the story of how He prepared her for me, but also how He prepared me for her.

When the oldest of my five children was fourteen and the youngest six, we bought one-way tickets to Ethiopia to do a year-long internship with an organisation that worked with orphaned children. There were varying emotions within the family about going. Some resented leaving our homeland, some were uncertain about timing, while others saw it as an adventure. I saw it as the opportunity to help those who were broken.

What I didn't know was that I was the one who was about to be restored. It was there, in Ethiopia, that I discovered who I really was and just how much God loved me. God used Ethiopia to set me free, not just externally, but internally. As one year turned to two, I quickly realised that although I had arrived determined to change their world, it was my world, my inner world, that I needed to work on first. The reality is that it is only when we have learned to nurture and feed the soil that produces the fruit in our own lives that we are able to feed those on the outside.

From the time we are born, we start to construct a framework—much like that of a planter box—for what we fill our lives with. This framework seeks to engage with every decision we make, deciphering who we trust, what we believe and how we behave. With each tragedy and triumph, a conclusion is drawn and nailed into the structure that we build as our truth. Sometimes that can be a good thing, but when trauma has distorted your view of the world and God, (like it had mine), our lives can become subject to the limitations those belief systems place around us. Instead of us exercising power over them, they exert power over us.

This is a system that we are all subject to, a progression from our spirit, to our soul and then our body. When we think about our holistic make up, that framework can represent our spiritual being, which we then fill with our soul issues (our heart) which becomes the soil. From this soil, our decisions are made, which are then outworked with our body. Too often we draw conclusions about people by what we see them do—their actions. We form labels about what type of people we think they are. It is not until you hear their story, unpack the circumstances that formed their framework and the trauma that formed the soil of what their behaviour grew out of, that you can truly understand who they are.

Our Creator never intended our lives to be limited by our pain, but unfortunately it is often when we are in the middle of our pain, that we make agreements that form how we understand the world. That's why He reminds us to: "Trust in the Lord with all your heart and lean not on your own understanding" (Proverbs 3:5)—because our understanding can fall to pieces in a minute, but He will never fall apart. He designed us to live in a wide-open space, not a confined planter box. He invites us to open our hearts to Him, so that He can restore us back to the garden.

As I share part of my story and invite you to reflect on yours, I want to challenge you not to focus on your behaviour, but rather to look at the garden—to see the bigger picture of what God intended for us from the beginning.

Yes, sometimes He will require us to go back in order to move forward. This is always true of the restorative process, because the definition of 'restoration' is, "the action of returning something to a former owner, place or condition." It is like the process of restoring a building or work of art to its original condition.

Remember, you were created for the garden. When you look back over your life, be ready to deconstruct some of what you have held to be true for far too long.

GOD'S BLUEPRINT

In the big picture of the creation narrative, we get a glimpse of how God intended our life on earth to look through the garden. Yet, there is a specific blueprint that He also had for you before you were even born! Psalm 139 tells us that we were woven together, that all the days of our lives were ordained and written in God's book before one of them even came to be (vv. 15-16). This blueprint was complex—a holistic framework to be filled with your genetics, culture, and personality; affected by the time, location, and family you were born into.

Knowing this was all going to be sabotaged and broken, Jesus stepped in and made an announcement. Standing in the Synagogue on this historic Sabbath day, He began His earthly ministry by declaring His prophetic place:

> *The Spirit of the Lord is upon me, because he has anointed me to proclaim good news to the poor. He has sent me to proclaim liberty to the captives and recovering of sight to the blind, to set at liberty those who are oppressed, to proclaim the year of the Lord's favor.*
>
> Luke 4:18-19, ESV

Jesus was reading from what we know as the sixty-first book of Isaiah—it was the scheduled reading in the scrolls for that particular day, and here He was, claiming it as His own, pronouncing His purpose on the earth. He followed the reading by announcing, "What you have just heard me read has come true today" (v. 21).

While we tend to view His anointing as a mandate to minister to different groups of people, I believe there is room for us to believe that

He was also speaking about proclaiming good news to every part of *the one*—that He was sent to restore every part of us—and in so doing, He acknowledged our holistic makeup.

Too often we ignore the different dimensions of our existence and only focus on one aspect of our being. Yet we do an injustice to our Creator and a disservice to those created in His image when we fail to recognize that people are a multi-faceted race who have a multiplicity of needs our Father desires to restore.

When we spiritualize everything, we forfeit the obligation we have to maintain and improve other aspects of who we are. We can live under condemnation for things that aren't spiritual but rather physical or psychological. Though these three components are intertwined, we have to discern which elements are coming into play in order to tend to the right part of our garden. When we have the ability to see things in a holistic manner, it liberates us to assign responsibility to the appropriate aspect of our being—perhaps our dysfunction has less to do with our spiritual walk and more to do with our psychological and social. If we see everything as spiritual, then we can find ourselves blaming God for the evil that is going on around us and pay little attention to the other relevant factors. The story of Job is a good example of this.

THE CASE STUDY OF JOB

When we first meet Job, we find him prospering in every area of his life. He has a thriving business, a loving family, good standing in the community, physical strength, mental stability, and a healthy fear of God. The scene is set in Job 1:

> *In the land of Uz there lived a man whose name was Job. This man was blameless and upright; he feared God and shunned evil. He had seven sons and three daughters, and he owned seven thousand sheep, three*

> *thousand camels, five hundred yoke of oxen and five hundred donkeys, and had a large number of servants. He was the greatest man among all the people of the East.*
>
> Job 1:1-3

Of all the people of the East, Job stood out. He didn't just stand out to the people of the day, he stood out to God. So much so, that when Satan told God about how he had been roaming the earth, God started to brag about Job. Even *He* told Satan how amazing Job was, and how there was no one like him on the earth. Satan took that up as a challenge—he had seen how God was blessing Job and attributed his fear of God to all God had done for him. So, God gave him power over all that Job had, along with permission to strike it *all* provided he did not lay a finger on Job himself (Job 1:9-12).

His livestock, his servants, his buildings, and his children were the first to go. Still Job remained steadfast in his confession of faith, so Satan appealed to God to also let him attack his flesh. God granted his request but commanded he spare Job's life. While Job was able to endure the loss of his material possessions and even the death of all his children, it was the loss of his physical strength that finally overwhelmed him. When his friends came to see Job, he was riddled with such extreme boils that they tore their robes and wept at his appearance.

Job was a mess.

At that point, Job's confession started to change—he almost sounded suicidal and at one stage even begins to blame God: "He would ... multiply my wounds for no reason. He would not let me catch my breath, but would over whelm me with misery" (Job 9:17-18). His declining reputation in the community was clearly communicated to him by his judgmental friends who soon convinced Job that the situation he found himself in was his sole responsibility.

Psychologically, financially, physically, spiritually, socially, and vocationally, Job had lost almost everything. There was no respite from the pain he was feeling, and he mourned the existence he had experienced before. Yet God was still watching Job, taking note of how he was responding to the traumatic events surrounding him, and He stepped in to bring perspective.

After declaring His sovereignty and reminding Job of all the amazing feats He had accomplished, God rebuked Job's friends and challenged their theories. With a renewed vision of God's greatness and His attention to every detail, Job responds in humble repentance and adoration:

> *I know that you can do all things; no purpose of yours can be thwarted. You asked, 'Who is this that obscures my plans without knowledge?' Surely I spoke of things I did not understand, things too wonderful for me to know.*
>
> Job 42:2-3

The beauty of this story is that Job came out of his trial with a greater understanding of the nature of God; his reverence for God went to new levels as he saw what he had never seen before. As the writer of Hebrews expresses, everything that could have been shaken, was shaken, so that what could not be shaken would remain for Job (Hebrews 12:27).

As a result of his repentance and confession of renewed faith, Job was restored in every area of his life. We see him coming back into a social community and receiving relational restitution with the birth of more children, renewed financial blessing, doubled vocational compensation, physical healing, and a healthy state of mind.

> *After Job had prayed for his friends, the Lord restored his fortunes and gave him twice as much as he had before. All his brothers and sisters and everyone who had known him before came and ate with him in his house.*

They comforted and consoled him over all the trouble the Lord had brought on him, and each one gave him a piece of silver and a gold ring.

Job 42:10-11

Even though the Bible makes no mention of what happened in the years between the first half of his life and his better, latter half, we have to assume there was work involved on Job's part in this process of restoration. Work in forgiving his friends (God actually addressed the toxicity in their relationship and called them to repent but also gave Job the task of praying for them); work in restocking his fields with animals and growing the crops to feed them; work in rebuilding his barns and houses; and working through the deepest loss of all—that of his children. But in all of these things, God's hand was upon him, and "the Lord blessed the latter part of Job's life more than the former part" (Job 42:12).

In the larger scope of things, this is our story, too. Before we were even thought of by our parents, God had thought of us. He had bragged about us and planned out our days, wanting to accelerate the blessings on our lives. But the enemy stepped in and intervened. He took the first opportunity in the Garden of Eden to penetrate the hedge of protection God had originally established for us. Every area of our being was held hostage by his schemes. But God had a redemption plan all along. He, the Word made flesh, came to dwell among us and bring everything back into order (John 1).

Jesus burst into the scene, approaching the Jews in the Synagogue and doing with them what God had done with Job's friends: He brought truth to their preconceived ideas of what they thought He was like. They were religious naysayers who only paid attention to the religious law that applied to their spiritual wellbeing. But Jesus was there to proclaim that there was more to life than just obeying a set of rules—more to attend to than simply our spiritual health.

A HOLISTIC REDEMPTION PLAN

In Luke 4, we find the account of Jesus standing in the temple as He read the prophetic words of Isaiah 61. Interestingly, the two renditions of the passage are not identical. Luke's record has no mention of the words, "He has sent me to bind up the brokenhearted," and it also carries the added mention of "recovery of sight for the blind." However, when we combine both texts, we discover that Jesus was in fact, announcing restoration for every aspect of our holistic makeup: "Good news to the poor"—which addresses our financial health; "bind up the brokenhearted"—speaking of our mental health; "freedom for the captives"—appealing to our social wellbeing, then Jesus speaks of "recovery of sight for the blind" which represents our physical health; "release from darkness for the prisoners" creating a connection to our spiritual health before He sets out to "proclaim the year of the Lord's favour" which I believe appeals to our vocational health.

Why was it necessary for God to send Jesus to restore every part of our lives? Because in the garden, every aspect of humanity was affected by the Fall!

Financially, blessing was stripped from Adam and Eve as they were displaced from the garden, their place of abundant provision.

Physically, Eve had to now bear children in pain.

Socially, the relationship between these newlyweds became strained under the pressure of blame and brokenness.

Psychologically, before the Fall, their minds were free of condemnation and shame, yet this one act caused them to clothe themselves and hide away because of shame for the first time.

Vocationally, Adam's life became more arduous as his hobby of tending to the garden became a sweat-breaking chore.

Spiritually, their relationship with God was fractured and resulted in a death of what was, which created the framework for what now is and forever will be.

There's a process by which each of these areas can be restored by God, but they are also not in and of themselves disconnected. They are all intertwined within holistic creations, created by a holistic Godhead. Each aspect of the restoration calls us to work for the ground we need to take back, but God establishes a way to do it and invites us to join Him in the process.

When God started to make plans to restore what sin had come to take away, He went *all out!* Like He did with Job when he came to the end of himself and was mourning in deep darkness, God sought to restore *all* that we had lost. That day in the synagogue, Jesus pronounced the hope He had come to bring in place of the deep darkness that swept the earth. Further on in Isaiah 61, we're told the outcome of Christ's restorative work will be to:

... provide for those who grieve in Zion—
to bestow on them a crown of beauty instead of ashes,
the oil of joy instead of mourning,
and a garment of praise instead of a spirit of despair.
They will be called oaks of righteousness,
a planting of the Lord for the display of his splendor.

Isaiah 61:3

The word 'ashes' here, translates from a Hebrew word that denotes a sense of worthlessness. *A crown of beauty for ashes*, indicates that God wants to lift our heads out of a place of feeling unworthy; for our mourning to be replaced by the oil of joy as we experience His work of restoration. Like Job, when we come to know God, we discover who we truly are and find our sense of identity in Him. Yet, like Job, there is often some wrestling and work that we need to do *with God* to restore the aspects of our being that have been broken.

If you've heard the gospel at any point in your life, you should know that Jesus was God's solution for the Fall—that God sent His

Son to pay the price of sin so we could have eternal life. And while I am not diminishing the wonder of the gift of salvation, sometimes we are so focused on the eternal life He came to bring, that we forget about the abundant life He came for as well. When Jesus called out the destructive work of the enemy, He simultaneously declared:

> *I came that they may have **life**, and have it **abundantly**.*
>
> John 10:10, ESV

Jesus did not come just for the soul and spirit, but for life—and life in abundance! This is His invitation to you even *today*.

🌿 YOUR INVITATION INTO THE GARDEN

When: *did you make an agreement about your future, based on the pain of your past?*

Where: *can you see the original version of you wanting to burst through?*

What: *area can you invite Jesus to help you find restoration for today?*

CHAPTER TWO

The River

God's Flow

In Addis Ababa, the capital of Ethiopia, flows a river. I remember one rainy season walking across a bridge that ran over it and noticing the contrast between the two sides of the river. On one bank was the road that led up to the city dump, lined with vegetation where locals planted seeds. Above the planted area were the slum houses where people lived. The slum-people would wash their clothes in the dirty river, then lay them out on bank of the river to dry. Directly on the other side of the river, were the diplomatic mansions. I often thought of the slum-dwellers looking across the bank to the wealthy diplomats, and the diplomats also, looking out their windows to the slums. In that city, it was a picture of two worlds, with a river running right through it.

WHEN WE SOLD OUR HOUSE IN AUCKLAND to get ready to go to Ethiopia, fear set in. We incurred unexpected costs to bring the house up to building standards and lost a lot of money in the process. With nothing tying us to New Zealand, we wondered if we'd made the right decisions. *Had we made a huge mistake?* The fear of getting it wrong—of failure—nearly stopped us from leaving. Had we allowed it to, it would have stopped us from both receiving the blessings that lay ahead for us in Ethiopia, and from *being* the blessing that God desired us to be.

In Psalm 46, the psalmist writes:

> *There is a river whose streams make glad the city of God, the holy place where the Most High dwells. God is within her, she will not fall; God will help her at break of day.*
>
> Psalm 46:4-5

Fear of failure is probably one of the biggest hindrances to our growth. Perhaps you read those words, "she will not fall" and you think, *impossible.* You just *know* you're going to fail and fall again. It is this lie from the enemy (also called "the accuser of our brothers and sisters" in Revelation 12:10), that makes us believe we're not worth the risk God took to invest His assignment in us. But the reason we can confidently step out to do the things God is calling us to do, is because He is within us—His 'river', the Holy Spirit runs through us.

A river is a conduit from one source of water to another; a natural flowing watercourse. When we trace this imagery through Scripture, we see that the Garden of Eden was watered by a river (Genesis 2:10). But with the fall, we not only lost access to the garden, we also lost access to the river. Revelation 22:1 tells us that when Eden is restored, we will see, "the river of the water of life, as clear as crystal, flowing from the throne of God and of the Lamb." God showed the prophet Ezekiel what this restoration would look like, allowing him to see the water that flowed out of the temple (Ezekiel 47). But somewhere in the middle, between the penultimate restoration of Eden and where we sit in history right now, the dispensation of the Holy Spirit allows us to believe that as we are the temple, that God wants this river—the river of living water—to flow out of us.

Ezekiel's vision shows us what the impact of allowing the Holy Spirit to flow through us can mean for the world:

> *He asked me, 'Son of man, do you see this?' Then he led me back to the bank of the river. When I arrived there, I saw a great number of trees on each side of the river. He said to me, 'This water flows toward the eastern region and goes down into the Arabah, where it enters the Dead Sea. When it empties into the sea, the salty water there becomes fresh. Swarms of living creatures will live wherever the river flows. There will be large numbers of fish, because this water flows there and makes the salt water fresh; so where the river flows everything will live.'*
>
> Ezekiel 47:6-9

Created in the image of God, we have the ability to bring life to dead situations because the Spirit of God is the source of all we do. There is absolutely no limit to what God can do for us and through us, if we will see His power for what it is and have confidence in our ability to draw from it.

FROM GRIEF TO HOPE

We live in a world that is mourning. The Covid pandemic has left no one untouched and there is a collective, global grief for the way life once was—for the people, jobs, opportunities, and freedoms we once loved and held. So heavy has the grief been for many, that their only way of escape has been to end their own lives or the lives of others; suicide rates, domestic violence, and acts of rage have increased.

Isaiah 61 reminds us that Jesus came to "comfort all who mourn and provide for those who grieve" (vv. 2-3). So what if we allowed for grief to be something more than just the emotion we feel at the loss of a loved one? What if we let it encompass the unmet expectations that we hold for ourselves or for others? For the reality that life is not what we hoped it would be—that *we* are not who we hoped to be in this season of our lives? If we could acknowledge where we are grieving, then we would open ourselves up to the solution Jesus has provided; we could move from grief to hope.

There was a point in my life where I had to grieve the father I always wished I had. My father suffered from mental illness throughout my childhood, and facing the reality of his condition—growing to understand the psychological effects of a chemical imbalance in the brain—meant accepting I couldn't change him. I couldn't make him the father I wanted him to be. But even if his mental health couldn't be fully restored, there was still hope for our relationship to be restored if I could let go of the expectation for him to be someone he was incapable of being.

Just like the fear of failure, unprocessed grief can hinder us from becoming the conduit of living water that God wants us to be. But these aren't the only things that can block the flow of the Holy Spirit in our lives—in every part of our makeup there are things that seek to restrict out capacity. However, just as Ezekiel was taken into the river and saw it grow its capacity to be filled with more water, so, too, can we build our capacity for God to pour into our lives, so that we can pour more out.

But first, we must address the issues that create blockages to the flow of God. This brings us back to the holistic model of Luke 4 and Isaiah 61.

IDENTIFYING BLOCKAGES

Shame (Psychological)

Shame buries our potential and acts like a tomb for our authentic self. Brené Brown (an American social worker who studies shame and vulnerability in human connection) describes it as "The intense painful feeling or experience of believing that we are flawed and therefore unworthy of love and belonging." Yet scripture gives us a hope that takes us beyond our shame.

> *Instead of your shame* you will receive a ***double portion**, and **instead of disgrace** you will **rejoice in your inheritance**. And so you will inherit a double portion in your land, and **everlasting joy will be yours**.*
>
> Isaiah 61:7

Shame and disgrace are results of our internal beliefs, the expectations of others, and our behaviour. I have had my own journey with shame and it has often won me over. But as I've come to understand my identity in Christ, I have realised my behaviour is not attached to my identity, therefore, neither can be my shame.

In a season where I found myself self-protecting and trying to escape people because of the shame I carried, I sat and wrote this letter overlooking the Sydney Harbour:

> *Today I say goodbye to shame. Especially to the shame that tries to bind me to the event that took place here in Darling Harbour two years ago. The shame that tries to tell me that I failed, that I heard wrong; that I'm not good enough or pretty enough or not even worthy of love. That shame, I hear you, but I'm not listening to you anymore. You're a liar and a thief. You stole my joy but I'm taking it back. You took my confidence but I'm reclaiming it now. You lied about my worth but the truth has set me free. I know the truth now. I am loved.*

I am worthy. I was right—not because of the outcome, but because I chose courage over fear. I chose authenticity over fake appearances. I chose love over loneliness. I chose to obey rather than to disbelieve. And for that, I'm a better me. A more authentic Michelle, and I have found my identity. I am that Proverbs 31 woman who sees a field and stakes a claim on it. Whether I win or lose, at least I bid. And bidders are always winners because they leave with no regrets of not trying.

I had taken a risk in that season; I had allowed myself to be vulnerable, and had been rejected. But with that letter, the blockage of shame gave way.

Secrets (Social)

Within authentic relationships there needs to be transparency and vulnerability—and to protect these, there also needs to be discretion. But discretion is different to keeping secrets, especially the 'skeleton in the closet' type secret. While Ecclesiastes 3:7 reminds us that there is a "time to be silent and a time to speak", there are times when staying silent hinders our flow and our growth.

In his book, *Healing the Child Within*, Charles Whitfield, says,

Shame-based families often, though not always, have a secret. This secret may span all kinds of 'shameful' conditions, from family violence to sexual abuse to alcoholism to having been in a concentration camp. Or the secret may be as subtle as a lost job, a lost promotion or a lost relationship. Keeping such secrets disables all members of the family, whether or not they know the secret (Fischer, 1985). This is because being secretive prevents the expression of questions, concern and feelings (such as fear, anger, shame and guilt). And the family thus cannot communicate freely. And the 'child within' each family member remains stifled—unable to grow and to develop.

Family secrets are all too often passed off as 'the way it has to be,' and we fail to understand the consequences of festering secrets. One of these consequences is that we can feel held captive by the secrets we have to keep. Jesus wants to restore us socially by bringing liberty to the places where we feel captive in this way—to where secrets have kept us bound.

A natural recipe for social discord includes the prevention of questions, concerns, and feelings. In contrast, there is a natural flow when we are free to verbally process the ideas and situations that occur in our lives by asking questions, expressing concerns, and openly discussing them in a safe environment.

If we have been manipulated or coerced into 'keeping our opinion to ourselves' or 'minding our own business,' our development is stifled; emotional intelligence is crippled and this then seeps into other areas of our lives. Self-worth is diminished when we put others' needs before our own in unhealthy ways, and confusion, depression, and anxiety take up residence when the thoughts circle around our minds with no outlet to release them.

King David had a moment where he experienced this reality, and his words show us the impact of staying silent:

> *When I kept silent, my bones wasted away through my groaning all day long. For day and night your hand was heavy on me; my strength was sapped as in the heat of summer.*
>
> Psalm 32:3-4

David spoke up and had a conversation with God. He exemplified the importance of speaking out what is burning in your heart. As we speak out, or flow out, what has entered into our being at every gateway, we turn over and bring to life what can block us up.

We can see this connection happen spiritually as well.

Sin (Spiritual)

Sin can also become a blockage to our flow because ultimately, sin is to disobey God. If God tells us that something is right or wrong and we don't believe Him, then we find ourselves sinning against Him. James put it like this: "If anyone, then, knows the good they ought to do and doesn't do it, it is sin for them" (James 4:17). God, however, provided the antidote for our sin through His Son, a perfect, unblemished, sacrificial lamb. He made "Him who had no sin to be sin for us, so that in Him we might become the righteousness of God" (2 Corinthians 5:21).

God already did the work for us to be made righteous, but there is a process that needs to happen in order for what He has done to clear the blockage and restore our spirit. We find this processed outlined in Romans 10:8-13:

> *But what does it say? 'The word is near you; it is in your mouth and in your heart', that is, the message concerning faith that we proclaim: If you declare with your mouth, 'Jesus is Lord,' and believe in your heart that God raised him from the dead, you will be saved. For it is with your heart that you believe and are justified, and it is with your mouth that you profess your faith and are saved. As Scripture says, 'Anyone who believes in him will never be put to shame.' For there is no difference between Jew and Gentile—the same Lord is Lord of all and richly blesses all who call on him, for, 'Everyone who calls on the name of the Lord will be saved.'*

The process of restoration starts with the Word entering our hearts and mouths through our ears (v. 8). Later, in this same chapter, Paul would go on to tell us that "faith comes by hearing, and hearing by the word of God" (v. 17). But what has been 'heard' and 'received' must then be confessed because it is when we "confess with our mouth" what we "believe in our heart" that we will be saved (v. 9).

Through our confession, the Word that has entered our heart comes alive as it is spoken out. This is why James tells us that, "faith by itself, if it is not accompanied by action, is dead" (James 2:17). It is the works—the confession or the outworking of what we believe—that activates our faith. It is much like applying for a bank account and receiving a debit card in the mail. Usually, it arrives with some instructions about how you can activate the card so you can access what is inside the account. In the same way, we can have the idea of God in our head, or read in His Word about what we need to do, but it's not until we act on it that our spirit is restored.

In these verses, Paul gave the Roman believers clear instructions about how they could turn what they have heard into a life-giving event. If they were willing to take a stand and confess that this *man* they had crucified and buried was actually the *Messiah*, the fruit of their obedience to what God was saying, would be holistic reprieve.

There would be *psychological restoration*: "Anyone who believes in him will never be put to shame" (v. 11).

There would be *social restoration*: "For there is no difference between Jew and Gentile—the same Lord is Lord of all and richly blesses all who call on him" (v. 12).

There would be *spiritual restoration:* "Everyone who calls on the name of the Lord will be saved" (v. 13).

So, what do *we* do with sin? 1 John 1:9 says: "If we confess our sins, he is faithful and just and will forgive us our sins and purify us from all unrighteousness." Like Paul exhorted his audience to confess what they had heard and believed, we, too, must confess what we have done. Only then will we be able to know the restoration to righteousness that the Father always intended for us.

Selfishness (Financial)

In Matthew's gospel, Jesus exhorts us with these words:

> *Do not store up for yourselves treasures on earth, where moths and vermin destroy, and where thieves break in and steal. But store up for yourselves treasures in heaven, where moths and vermin do not destroy, and where thieves do not break in and steal. For where your treasure is, there your heart will be also.*
>
> Matthew 6:19-21

This Scripture highlights two things in the context of holistic restoration. Firstly, there is a direct connection between how you spend your money and what is in your heart (your mindset or beliefs, values, and priorities), and secondly, there is a direct connection between where you invest your money and the impact you have in eternity.

Because of the holistic nature of our finances, we need a holistic antidote to unblock the flow. By 'holistic nature' I mean that money is not an entity unto itself. The motivation behind why you spend your money, and the social, spiritual, and physical impact on how you choose to spend it, renders it multi-dimensional. Therefore, the way to keep the flow going with your finances and to see the financial situation in your life restored, is not about where or how you invest your money, but your heart.

Proverbs 4:23 says, "Above all else, guard your heart, for everything you do flows from it." When we don't guard our heart against selfish motives and the culture of this world, we can easily find ourselves on the downward spiral of debt and financial restriction. If we can see God's provision rather than our own, place others' needs above ours, and treat money as a tool to be used to build His Kingdom, then money will no longer have a grip on us. A poverty mindset tells us that we don't have enough, and therefore we need to keep as much of it in our bank account as we can. This blocks the flow of what God wants to do, not just with our money, but also with our lives. As we take Him at His Word (and His Word has plenty to say about finances), then we will see our finances flourish. Although Luke 6:38 refers primarily to the 'measure' with which we judge others, it perfectly articulates this principle: "Give, and it will be given to you. A good measure, pressed down, shaken together and running over, will be poured into your lap. For with the measure you use, it will be measured to you."

As you give and don't withhold, you will see your finances restored as well as your relationships (selflessness is attractive!), and ultimately, your heart.

Stagnation (Physical)

We were never meant to be stagnant. We were designed for movement because we are created in the image of a God who is always on the move; always working and roaming about. We are "his offspring", and in Him, we "live and move and have our being" (Acts 17:28). However, modern inventions have made it easier for us to sit around and stifle the movement that is meant to be recreating the cells within our bodies.

The average adult body is made up of sixty percent water. Now we all know if we leave a cup of water sitting for an extended amount of time, it starts to become stinky; it becomes a breeding ground for bacteria to grow. The same is true of our bodies. If we don't move around, we become a breeding ground for sickness and disease to grow. Whether it is walking, stretching, running, boxing, or dancing, we need to find ways to move our bodies and keep the restoration process going. We also need to fuel our bodies with good nutrients and the right amount of vitamins and minerals—when we eat well, we can exercise and function to the best of our ability. Solomon, the wisest man to live, penned these words to caution us against stagnation:

> *Go to the ant, you sluggard; consider its ways and be wise! It has no commander, no overseer or ruler, yet it stores its provisions in*

summer and gathers its food at harvest. How long will you lie there, you sluggard? When will you get up from your sleep? A little sleep, a little slumber, a little folding of the hands to rest— and poverty will come on you like a thief and scarcity like an armed man.

Proverbs 6:6-11

The ant illustrates for us the importance of movement to stay physically well *and* in order to prosper financially. But sometimes, we need some help to not only get physically moving, but also to know what it is we are meant to be doing—what our vocation is.

Self (Vocational)

Preconceived ideas, family expectations, misconstrued motives, or plain insecurity—these are all ways that *we* can become the blockage to our own vocational flow. I heard it once said that insecurity is another form of pride, and I fully believe that to be true, because what insecurity does is places an emphasis on 'I' and not on the One who we can do all things through: God. Words like, "I can't", "I'm not good enough", and "I could never…" are all prefaces to excuses as to why we can't do what we may have a deep longing in our heart to do. You were created to do something specific. Your vocation itself may not necessarily be what you were born to do, but it might be how you finance the calling on your life. There is something about the way you were wired, the passions you have, and the sphere of influence in which you exist, that work together to bring you satisfaction in a way nothing else can.

* * *

Revelation 22:2 tells us that the leaves of the trees Ezekiel saw lining the banks of the river, are for the "healing of the nations." As we work with the Holy Spirit to remove the things that block Him flowing freely in and through us, we, the trees of God's planting, play a part in God's plan to bring wholeness to all people.

🌿 YOUR INVITATION INTO THE GARDEN

When: *have you felt like you were living in the flow?*

Where: *do you need to unblock the flow in an area mentioned in this chapter?*

What: *can you do to help bring restoration to others?*

CHAPTER THREE

The Dirt

God's Place of Rest

In Ethiopia we lived in a fertile region with good, rich soil that produced bountiful crops. In the dry season, the ground would harden within days, then crack, but in the rainy season, the soil became dark brown, thick, and heavy. No matter how hard we tried to avoid it, it got on our shoes and pants. With no washing machine, a lady would come to wash our clothes with a bucket. But the water would soon be dirty, so she had to handwash our clothes multiple times to get all the dirt out. The dirt in our region was also known to hold a bug. If it got into people's feet, they often developed elephantitis. As a result, people were very cautious, and every home had a bucket of water at the front door so people could wash their feet whenever they got dirty.

WE ARE ALL BUT DIRT. We came from dried up dirt, and we will return to dirt. The psalmist tells us, "As a father has compassion on his children, so the Lord has compassion on those who fear him, for he knows how we are formed, he remembers that we are dust" (Psalm 103:13-14).

In the darkness of the soil, an environment exists fundamentally to nurture growth. Resurrection growth transpires as dead seeds are buried for a period of time, allowing them to burst open into a new, transformed version of what they looked like when they entered the soil. Life is a process of growth—but just like the seed, our own growth often happens in the darkest of seasons. The mystery of the process stretches us to believe that something of transcendence is taking place even in the darkest of our life experiences.

I remember the first time I experienced darkness. It was when I reached up for my mother's hand as I stood beside her in the reception area of the psychiatric hospital where my father had been admitted—it was to be the first of many visits and admissions. The hospital was not only dark physically, there was also a spiritual darkness that resided there. The musty smell of this old building and the fear that it aroused had me wanting out.

The effects of my father's mental illness on our family were extensive. Not only was he physically unable to care for us because he was frequently in hospital or crippled by the effects of his medication, but his struggle to hold down a job left him vocationally futile and financially frustrated—unable to provide for many of our material needs. His lack of social intelligence brought shame, and his mental instability left us void of any sense of safety and security. All of these things robbed us of a deep connection with him, and they each affected my worldview, helping to construct a 'planter box' around my life in my formative years.

The formative years for a child are between birth and eight years of age. It is in these years that the foundation is laid for the rest of our lives. Like soil that needs to be well cared for and tended, so, too, does a child need the most love and attention during these years. There is no other period of time in our lives where physical, cognitive, social, and emotional growth is more rapid.

These are the years that establish the foundation for what will grow from our lives. We start our formative years full of confidence. We can hold the gaze of the one who held us, allowing them to see into our heart, and we're not afraid to allow people to know our needs—whether we're hungry or uncomfortable. Vulnerability is our strongest point because we are often naked and unashamed. However, when the love and care that an infant requires isn't assigned in the proper way, there is a stunting of the growth and development in that child that will exist until it is healed and restored.

ESCAPING THE DARKNESS

When soil is being prepared by the farmer or gardener for sowing, they can take it through a process called 'fallowing.' The practice of fallowing is when the gardener ploughs and harrows through the soil, breaking it open and turning it over with his tools. Then he will let it settle for a period of time, to allow the soil to become productive again. A waiting period happens where no seeds are to be sown, while the ground restores its fertility.

The things I experienced as a child because of my father's mental state, were like a fallowing. They broke me and rendered me prime real estate for a Healer to come along and nurture the broken places in my soul. But in the waiting period, I escaped to a fantasy world.

Whenever we visited my father, we would congregate in the common room of the hospital and my mother would pull up the seat at the piano and play. "Dream, dream, dream . . . when I want you, all I have to do is dream," she sang. I sometimes think that's where the dreaming started for me. I am a dreamer, but the only problem was, I was "dreaming my life away." Reality was so easily displaced by a fantasy world that I hoped would one day exist for me. This fantasy was my way of filling the empty, unstable vortex that existed in my soul. Living a life disengaged from reality was much more pleasant and comfortable than fully experiencing the tainted truth of my existence. In psychology, they call this dissociation.

The dark, depressed reality that I lived in, created a desire for comfort to erase the pain and moments of despair. So I created an alternative reality, a version of life I engaged with for comfort. Fantasy trumped reality and these fantasies became good stories I could use in spaces like 'show and tell' at school where I had little I was proud to share.

When we've experienced brokenness, when we feel lost, disillusioned, like we've messed up (or are messed up), when life feels hopeless and it seems like nothing is happening and nothing is changing, waiting for our soil to become productive again can feel difficult. Escapism can feel much more inviting. This is when God wants to restore our rest, because rest is vital to the healing process.

ENTERING INTO REST

> "The soil is the great connector of lives, the source and destination of all. It is the healer and restorer and resurrector, by which disease passes into health, age into youth, death into life. Without proper care for it we can have no community, because without proper care for it we can have no life."
>
> —Wendell Berry

This quote refers to plant life, yet it is also true of humanity. We came from and will return to the 'soil'; this is what connects us. Not only do we all have dirt in our genetic makeup, we also have dirt in our stories—

glimpses or seasons of darkness where light beckons to penetrate and bring hope. Resting in this truth beckons us to release our desire to figure out "*why?*" Why have I experienced this darkness?

The dark room in a photography studio is the place where a negative is developed. Children are often scared of the dark. Perhaps they have a heightened awareness of the spiritual realm; they sense what exists in the unseen. Most adults are scared of a different kind of dark—the dark waiting rooms of life where we can't see the future. Yet perhaps it is in those dark rooms where our character is developed the most. We can rest and trust in the truth that "He has made everything beautiful in its time" (Ecclesiastes 3:11).

In every area of our holistic being, it is rest that breaks the power of our desire to control everything. Rest allows us to regain perspective of what is important in our lives. It begs us to ask the question "does it really matter?" I remember getting all worked up over a situation I was facing in my family and hearing the Spirit say, "if it doesn't matter in eternity, it doesn't really matter." Rest allowed me to let go of the desire to be right, and embrace the relationship which was of far more value.

Resting is not an event; it is a process. It requires us to relinquish control and trust in the natural processes that occur without our involvement. This is true in our finances when we relinquish control of our tithe and surrender our ability to control that part of our income, trusting that we will still have all we need. It is also true of forgiveness—when we forgive, we release judgment and the control we want to have over someone else by holding them ransom to our disappointment.

Rest is also an action. It often takes more discipline to rest than it does to work. Jesus role-modelled this for us when He pulled himself away to a quiet or lonely place (e.g. Mark 1:35), effectively socially distancing from others so He could be spiritually filled. He could have hung around people who would tell Him how amazing He was after He performed many miracles, but instead He retreated to find His worth in intimacy with the Father. He allowed His identity to be fostered by nurturing His relationship with the Father when it could have been assailed by the praises of people.

Recovery takes place in the process of rest. Physical rest allows the energy that would normally be exerted for muscle function to flow into your cell replication and restoration—that is why often a doctor's remedy for our sickness will simply be to rest. The 'new' phenomena of intermittent fasting (or any other type of fasting) is another method God established to rest our bodies. Through this process, stored fat cells are utilized and healthy cells are regenerated.

Jesus came so that we may enter into spiritual rest (Hebrews 4). And just as rest allows soil to become fertile again, resting in His finished work on our behalf and the truth of His love for us, allows our hearts to become fertile again, too.

THE FERTILISER OF LOVE

In the Garden of Eden, God designed untainted soil, a fertile and perfect ground for healthy plants to grow from. The fall of man turned the soil into dirt—devoid of life and the ability to produce it. From then on, there had to be additives for the soil to become fertile.

'Blood and bone' is what my father used in our garden at home when he prepared the soil for a vegetable patch. This fertilizer is made from animal slaughter-house waste products; the death of those animals helps produce life for the ground. My father loved to get his hands dirty. He would put together gardens and lay bricks for barbeque pits. He dug plots of ground to grow vegetables and fruit trees that would feed his family with the "sweat from his brow"; as he did so, it was a reminder of the curse placed on Adam (Genesis 3:17-18).

Jesus' blood, shed for us, became the means by which we could be washed of our sin—redeemed from its curse. He was God's great fertilisation plan for our hearts, restoring us back to intimate communion with God. Christ's love fills in the gaps that have been formed in the fallowing process. When there has been a stunting of growth because of trauma and abuse, applying the love of God demonstrated in Jesus, brings healing.

Love is what grows in the waiting, replacing what trauma fallowed. As soil provides nutrients for seeds to burst forth into new life, so love does the same for our hearts, our relationships, and life in general. If love is deeply ingrained into the soil, then the nutrients essential for our holistic growth and the growth of others are always present. Love grows confidence, security, a known value and worth, freedom, grace, peace, hope, charity, compassion, and beauty. Love always produces abundant, resilient, healthy lives.

Jesus has an innate ability to love us unconditionally. He loved regardless of our behaviour because love is the essence of who God is. 1 John 4:8 tells us that "God is love." It is in His nature to fill our hearts with His love, and when we are secure in that love, resilience is built within us to withstand trials. I sensed God's love for me as a child, but His perfect love had not yet entered fully into every nook and cranny of my heart.

The framework for which I experienced love came through a father, who like most religious fathers in the eighties, was free to exercise fear-based punishment for unruly behaviour. My strong will and cheeky tongue often resulted in a 'smack' or a belt being pulled out of my father's trousers to be used as a weapon against my body. Consequently, I learned to live in fear. Yet 1 John teaches us that love "drives out fear because fear has to do with punishment" (4:18). I had to learn that God was not a Father out to punish me; Jesus had already taken the punishment for me.

I have found in my own struggle with trusting God with *all* of my heart, that my inability to do so came as a result of my lack of a good frame of reference. I had subconsciously constructed a framework, a planter box that I could work from—one that told me I needed to do things independently; that I did not need someone to rely on. This belief was established because I had been unable to rely on my father as a child.

When the beliefs we hold are based on misconstrued ideals, potentially placed on us by the effects of the broken world we were born into, the framework that we operate from becomes dysfunctional. The fruit of what grows within that dysfunction is compounded when shame is added into the mix. What we fail to remember is that the six-year-old, or twelve-year-old (or whatever age you were when you were broken) version of us, was the one that made that planter box! The deception we may have been privy to, or the reality that we never asked to be a part of, shaped our beliefs. They become our own understanding that Proverbs 3:4-5 tells us not to lean on—for when we do, it will most likely fall apart. But when we trust in the Lord with all our heart, He will direct our paths.

2 Corinthians 10:4-5 tells us that pulling down strongholds in our minds is a necessary part of our growth. "The weapons we fight with are not the weapons of the world. On the contrary, they have divine power to demolish strongholds. We demolish arguments and every pretension that sets itself up against the knowledge of God, and we take captive every thought to make it obedient to Christ."

1 Samuel 12:22 says "For the sake of his great name the Lord will not reject his people, because the Lord was pleased to make you his own." This is in His nature—once you are His, He will not reject you or abandon you. He loves you deeply and His grace is sufficient for you in your weaknesses.

As love and grace beckon you to rethink your frame of reference, do the hard work to pull it apart. Stand back. Look at it. Remember the nails and the scars that it left. Feel the splinters of wood that sparked pain in the depths of your soul. Then release it slowly to the fire. Surrender it to the One who can turn the ashes of that painful frame into a beautiful masterpiece that will set in stone a new foundation for which you can see your world through renewed eyes. Rest in the One who takes what you can't control and puts it in the controlled environment of His love.

Create space for a new way of thinking about your worth. Paul writes in 2 Corinthians 10:5 that we should "take captive every thought" that doesn't align with how God thinks about us. God doesn't want us to be governed by toxic, external circumstances which fold and bend at our every whim; He designed us to be controlled by an inner spirit that will stand up against the temptations that surround us. Make Jesus your ultimate frame of reference for love and life! As you do, you will build a 'planter box' for your soil to become the place of resurrection growth that God always intended it to be.

# YOUR INVITATION INTO THE GARDEN

When: *did you go through a season of darkness and felt like there was a time of waiting that was necessary for you to become fertile again?*

Where: *did you sense that something was working behind the scenes, turning things around for your good?*

What: *have been the fertilizing components in your life's journey? How have those experiences helped you to grow?*

CHAPTER FOUR

The Weeds

Restoring Identity

One road we often walked along in Debre Zeit, our hometown in Ethiopia, ran along a large field that, during the rainy season, became a lake. Alongside the road, wild weeds grew so long you could hardly see through them. I remember the stench that often came from those weeds--the smell of dead hyenas. At night, when the sun would set and we had access to a vehicle, we would sometimes take the children to watch as other hyenas came to feed off the dead carcasses around the lake.

After our first year in Ethiopia had passed, the weeds of insecurity began to emerge in both mine and my husband's hearts. He became increasingly jealous, accusing me of liking a man if I even spoke to him, and a pattern emerged whereby he would make these accusations and then withdraw to see if I would act on these alleged attractions. Meanwhile, I began to wonder if I did indeed have an adulterous heart—the combination of my husband's distance from me and his inability to love me well had awakened in me a deep need to be valued. Consequently, when someone did show me attention or talk positively about me, I was attracted to them. God began to reveal how cluttered my heart had become, forcing me to confront why I was searching for affection.

In the journey of growth, not only will there be things that cause our 'flow' to be blocked, but there will also be weeds along the banks of our river that seem like they are there to inhibit our growth. Some, we will need to uproot, but others may serve a purpose if we will allow them to. In Matthew, Jesus told a parable, inviting us to see the kingdom of God and the 'weeds' through a different lens.

> *The kingdom of heaven is like a man who sowed good seed in his field. But while everyone was sleeping, his enemy came and sowed weeds among the wheat, and went away. When the wheat sprouted and formed heads, then the weeds also appeared. The owner's servants came to him and said, 'Sir, didn't you sow good seed in your field? Where then did the weeds come from?' 'An enemy did this,' he replied. The servants asked him, 'Do you want us to go and pull them up?' 'No,' he answered, 'because while you are pulling the weeds, you may uproot the wheat with them. Let both grow together until the harvest. At that time I will tell the harvesters: First collect the weeds and tie them in bundles to be burned; then gather the wheat and bring it into my barn.'*
>
> Matthew 13:24-30

The advice given by the owner in this parable seems flawed, especially if you hold to the belief that weeds will only ever stunt the growth of the plants around them. Weeds are ugly and often incessantly replicate themselves, choking the life out of the plant we want to grow. They seek to destroy the flowering of our intended garden—at least, this is what we've always thought. Can weeds really "grow together" with a wheat plant? How on earth could keeping them together be beneficial?

In reality, weeds aren't necessarily as bad for the garden as we assume them to be. According to one observer: "Weeds are nature's support crops and are vital to a healthy system. Now, there is a point in the beginning of our cash crop's life where we have to fight for its little life and take down the weeds, but once the cash crop is big enough to not be overpowered by the weeds, let them grow."

Let them grow?! First Jesus says so, then the experts in horticulture . . . so, why is it that we can let them grow?

In our lives, this metaphor of weeds can represent internal and external elements that impose on what is trying to grow in our life. External influences include political constraints, physical disabilities, societal prejudices, circumstances beyond our control, or people that we just don't get along with. Weeds can also be internal characteristics— struggles, inherited behaviours, or temptations we're prone to. These intruders placed around us or within us, can seem to be in the way, but the lessons nature teaches us about the role of weeds in the garden can also be applied to our lives.

A NEW PARADIGM

Weeds grow faster than most plants by design; their main purpose is to build soil. Some species of weeds, called pioneer species, not only grow fast, but they also produce carbon quickly. This carbon lasts a long time after they die, and helps build the structure of the soil and retain water. During their lifetime, weeds absorb certain nutrients from the soil—when they die, these are brought to the top and released as they compost.

The weeds might seem bigger than the fruit we desire to produce in our lives. But we have to trust the process, knowing that those weeds will force us to grow and build longevity in the soil of our hearts. When it feels like they are taking what we need from the world, it may turn out that when those things die out, what they leave behind forms a better foundation for life than what we would have had without them. Yes, although we often want to see the weeds die and fade into obscurity, the truth is they have the ability to add value to our lives.

I see this process playing out in my parenting all the time. Obviously, children are a blessing and I wouldn't want to live life without my children—I love them to pieces! But in the midst of our day to day lives, there are internal and external triggers that can make me feel like I'm suffocating. The tasks and the responsibilities of raising and training my children for life are often overwhelming, and especially as a single parent now raising teenagers, I find ugly parts of me resurfacing that I thought had long been dealt with. This resurfacing causes me to grow because I don't like what I'm seeing. It forces me to evaluate why I react or respond the way I do, and I am availed at every opportunity that stresses me out, to dig deeper for peace. I am compelled to display self-control when this inherent weed of rage wants to overtake me. And each time I win in these battles (and they're not always won), I get stronger in my resolve, and that particular fruit (from the Spirit who guides me) grows bigger.

Weeds not only enrich the soil, some cover and protect it. Weeds that protect our soil come in many forms, such as obstacles that hinder us from stepping into the line of fire, like the time when my crying baby wouldn't settle in the back seat of the car, so I had to pull over and breastfeed him while his dad took the wheel. Driving with a crying baby could possibly be one of the most stressful driving experiences! At nineteen I wasn't thinking about my legal obligations, his crying simply caused me to pull my boy from the very seat that would soon be impacted by an oncoming car at the next major intersection we would drive through. The impact from that vehicle smashed the window, scattering glass across his empty car seat. 'Weeds,' like crying babies, people stopping us to chat on the way to work, or bills that turn up unexpectedly when money was planned for other material desires, could actually be a protective covering to help keep us from damage or distractions that could have harmed us had they not been in the way.

Sometimes they protect us by providing shade; being exposed to the sun too soon can kill a plant. This is when weeds can serve a protective purpose, not only shading the plant from the sun, but also bearing the brunt of attacks from insects and allowing it to reach maturity. In seasons of my life where I have felt like I need to move forward and chase a dream in my heart, waiting has felt like an incessant weed. But sometimes, dreams need to sit beneath the shade of that 'weed' while the one carrying the dream develops a character that can withstand the exposure the dream will bring. Watching your dream die because it was birthed prematurely is more painful than the wait. That time spent in the 'shade' that keeps you from being exposed to your dream and the elements that will come against you once it is out in the open, is vital and necessary.

In His wisdom, God frequently allows us to go the long way around to protect us from ourselves. He did that with the Israelites in their great exodus from Egypt—He didn't lead them through the land belonging to the Philistines, even though it was shorter, because He knew if the Israelites faced war, "they might change their minds and return to Egypt" (Exodus 13:17). We have to believe that He will do the same for us; that He will lead us away from the battles He knows we are not yet ready to fight.

We have to expect that when we come into relationship with Jesus, the weeds will still exist, because bare soil is rare in nature; diversity is key. Plants work together, helping feed one another. And yes, even the weeds are part of this 'feeding', because ultimately each weed is a reaction to whatever deficiency the soil has.

IDENTIFYING DEFICIENCIES

We can often identify the deficiency in our hearts through situations that birth weeds which are detrimental to our growth. For example, if you are deficient of love, the 'weeds' that grow as a reaction to that might look like insecurity, depression, or enabling relationships. Being *too* nice, to the point that your efforts to 'help' others enable them to carry on irresponsible behaviour, is a reaction. Your assistance in their lives will always come at the expense of you taking care of your own life. This essentially comes out of a need to be needed, or in psychological terms, 'co-dependence.'

Then there are deep deficiencies that manifest in addictive behaviours. One such deficiency might be the innate desire to belong and to be accepted for who you are. It could also be that you haven't learnt how to regulate your emotions internally, so you start to use external methods to achieve that purpose. When you are deficient of belonging and acceptance (and in the skills to know how to regulate your emotions), rejection will surface like never before—perhaps as 'triggering feelings' that came as you were rejected as a child, or fits of rage that you were exposed to. Fearing those experiences will happen again, we can find ourselves trying to please others to avoid that pain of rejection.

Paul, the apostle who persecuted Christians under the pressure of his Jewish peers, encouraged his fellow converts in Galatia to be like him saying:

Am I now trying to win the approval of human beings, or of God? Or am I trying to please people? If I were still trying to please people, I would not be a servant of Christ.

Galatians 1:10

His 'now' moment came when he realised the desire for approval that used to drive him, and he challenged those reading his letter (and us) to address the same issues. No longer was he caught up in trying to please people; God's approval was all he needed.

The weeds the enemy planted to choke growth are the very thing God will use to grow us. Joseph, in the book of Genesis, is the perfect example of this truth. Although his brothers sold him off as a slave, he met them years later with a spirit of forgiveness, telling them, "You intended to harm me, but God intended it for good to accomplish what is now being done, the saving of many lives" (Genesis 50:20). When we overcome our deficiencies, we can then help others to do the same.

The experiences of our childhood are often triggered when we face a similar situation in our adulthood. In that moment, we have an opportunity to tend to that hurt, like a weed in the garden, so that we can grow into a mature, complete person.

Some years ago, I attended a story writing workshop with Dan Allender. There, he introduced this idea of going back into our 'trauma.' As I sat in the room of practitioners working with people caught up in human trafficking and prostitution, I was being awakened to my own sexual brokenness. Dan taught us there was usually a reason we were drawn to help these people, and it was often because we had trauma of our own. As I revisited trauma in my own story and reflected on my relationship with my father, I was able to identify the inappropriate things that had been said to me as I was growing up and see how the verbal-sexual abuse I had endured had caused me to devalue myself. I wrote in my notes: "Trauma begins to change to the degree that we grieve. How close to the grief will your faith allow you to go? To the degree you remain distant, is the degree it [trauma] remains in power."

When we allow ourselves to face our fears, admit they exist, then go back into the moments when they were birthed, we can allow perseverance to finish its work. Persevering through the hard work of dealing with the root issues that stunted our growth, ultimately brings wholeness and healing.

The beautiful passage of restoration in Isaiah 61 goes on to tell the story of hope as God brings beauty for our ashes. In verses 4-5, we can see what the outcome will be of the 'turning over' of our 'soil', and how God will accomplish it:

> *They will rebuild the ancient ruins and restore the places long devastated; they will renew the ruined cities that have been devastated for generations. Strangers will shepherd your flocks; foreigners will work your fields and vineyards.*

Here we see described the transformation from weakness to strength, from broken to whole, and from being beneficiaries to being those who benefit others. The weeds of poverty, blindness, brokenheartedness, captivity, and prison, were not allowed to choke God's people; they only made them sweeter.

That's just what weeds can do in the natural too—they produce sugars that feed your plant. The sugars they produce make leaves, flowers, and eventually fruit and seeds, but as much as fifty percent of those sugars get exuded though the roots to attract the microscopic organisms of the soil food web.

The weeds in our life have something that we need, which will sweeten us up. This is why James exhorts us to "Consider it pure joy . . . whenever you face trials of many kinds, because you know that the testing of your faith produces perseverance. Let perseverance finish its work so that you may be mature and complete, not lacking anything" (James 1:2-4). Through the experiences we face, and as we choose life and forgiveness in the midst of our trials, we become sweeter for it. And our temporary afflictions are seen for what they are—light, momentary and useful in comparison to the glory which awaits us (2 Corinthians 4:17).

When I think of my relationship with my dad now, and how sweet it actually is, I know it is because God had to do a work in me so that I could choose forgiveness and love. Hopelessness and depression were the weeds that sought to choke me out as a child; I struggled with not ever knowing whether the pain would end. Being free from that environment, however, has given me an empathy toward those who are in it. Without those personal experiences, I wouldn't know the pain of those who suffer with mental illness or have family members who do, and wouldn't be able to approach them with the sweet empathy that has been produced over the years.

As we identify our deficiencies, we must learn to distinguish between the weeds that are there to support our growth for a season and bring a sweetness to our stories, and the toxic weeds we need to uproot. Some species of weeds attack our lives like a lantana weed. The lantana weed is a common weed in Sydney, Australia, where I am living now. In fact, right outside the window where I sit writing this, a lantana is fully wrapped around a huge eucalyptus tree that sits on my neighbour's lawn. The weed has grown so much that you can't even tell it is not a part of the tree unless you look at it closely. The weed buds a beautiful flower and even creates a nice scent, but it still remains a weed—and not a useful one. In fact, if left uncontrolled, it can become so invasive that it threatens entire plantations.

In families and cultures, we will always find weeds—negative practices and behaviours—that reduce our ability to develop into all we were created to be. We may have accepted them as normal, allowing them to grow from generation to generation, but in the depths of our hearts, we know they weren't meant to be a part of our experience. Denying the existence of these weeds will not make them go away but will actually further their growth until they become an intrinsic part of how we see ourselves. These weeds become "a prolific invader" that threatens the family's future. I mean this in the sense that we produce after our own kind, and if we continue to perpetuate unhealthy cultures in our families, we will only produce further dysfunction instead of the growth we're longing for. Therefore, their existence needs to be confronted and addressed.

Often, I have found that when we confront the 'norm', people get offended. We guard our family and our culture like a lioness guards her cubs—even if that culture is unhealthy. Offence will often cause us to excuse, ignore, and reason with those detrimental parts of our culture too. Offence, often stemming from a culture of shame, then becomes the biggest obstacle to freedom and growth. Like a weed nurtured by pride and arrogance, offence wraps itself around our children who in turn become the ones who suffer. We project an image that looks beautiful and smells beautiful so people will see what we want them to see, but it is our children who will get choked up in the toxicity that is produced. Denial, delusion, and disconnection from our destructive ways will cause us to continually have to deal with the weeds those roots produce.

It is often in our 'winter seasons' when those weeds are fully fledged and grow beyond their normal development. But it is also *after* the winter that these weeds need to be pulled out. Experts tell us that when you go to pull out those unsightly intruders, it is best done when the soil is wet and the ground more workable. At this stage, the soil more readily releases the weed and it's easier to pull the roots out intact. If the roots remain in the ground, they actually produce twice as much weed as before!

As the Holy Spirit exposes sin and negative practices, we have the choice to rip them out of the root systems that undergird our value system. As we expose the evil of their foundation, love, not shame, is what will cover over the wound and bring healing. 1 Peter 4:8 tells us, "Above all, love each other deeply, because love covers over a multitude of sins."

UNCOVERING OUR IDENTITY

During a pivotal season of my life, I remember retreating to the garden to get some head space. I climbed up into a tree that had a vine from our fence all wrapped up around in it. I pulled the branches of the vine out of the tree for hours. Thick undergrowth had weaved its way so tightly around the tree that my effort became both a strenuous workout and a reflective time. The vine had covered up the tree so much that you couldn't tell what the tree looked like anymore, just like a weed does. Parts of the tree had started to die because the vine had choked all the life out of it as the tree was no longer exposed to the sun.

That tree would have never known freedom unless we had pulled the vine out from around the branches. The vine had reached out of its own space to occupy the space of the tree; attaching itself by a small connection point the tree had to the vine. How it got over and around the whole tree amazed me, as it was never meant to reach out that far into the garden.

Some weeds we need to accept as part of our story, but others, we need to dislodge with the help of Jesus and the Holy Spirit as He gives us discernment in this process. As I tried to pull the weed out of that tree, I realised I needed help with some strong vines that had wrapped too tightly around the tree.

Sin is much like that vine. It makes itself look beautiful, quickly attaching itself to our lives until it soon looks like it is part of who we are. As we try to untangle its hold on us, we have to be careful to differentiate between what is the behaviour and what is our identity. Our identity, knowing who we are, is so foundational to identifying the weeds that try to trap us into believing we are something or someone else. The word 'identity' comes from late Latin *identitas*, meaning, "same". It is the part of you that is not attached to anything that you do, or that you belong to. It is the non-variable version of you that may have become attached to weeds that have entwined around you, but at the core of your being, will always remain the same.

When we enter the world, we will have things added to us . . . like a name. Yet not every human being that is born on the planet, is given a name. Whether or not you have a name, your identity is still valid, because although a name may be valuable (and in some cultures more valuable than others), it is still a variable in terms of your identity. It doesn't make you who you are.

More things get added to us, like parents. Some of us get one parent when we are born, some get two, others get a whole village, while some end up in an orphanage. Does it change who we are at our core? No. That's not part of our core identity.

Down the track, some of us have an education added to us, but some of us don't. Some have the opportunity in childhood to experience activities like sports, performing arts, or clubs like Scouts. Many people get passionate about their ability to participate in these things, but they, too, are still simply variables on the spectrum of our lifestyle, adding to the equation but not subtracting from our identity. Intrinsically, we are still the same person whether or not we have the opportunity to participate in such activities.

In adulthood, some have further education added—trade skills, business training, degrees or doctorates. Doors can open to gain experience and qualifications, more things get added to our 'portfolio' of life, but they're just that, additions. And none of these additions make us more valuable at the core of who we are, because at any stage, those things could be taken away. Sickness and accidents can strip these opportunities from us; businesses and vocations can be thwarted by economic climates or poor financial management. Whether these things are added to us or taken away from us, they don't change the validity of the identity that was established at our conception.

Relationships may also be added to us. We are indeed created for relationship, and finding a life partner or having a strong group of friends certainly can add to the value of our human experience. But some of us have better interpersonal skills than others; some of us have had bad experiences and base our acquisition of new relationships on our former experiences, hindering the fullness of what could be added, but in the end, it's all still just a variable. Our relationship status does not define us.

Material possessions are another contributory factor. We might obtain material wealth by inheritance or we could be positioned in countries and companies that allow us to accumulate financial assets through hard work. Some are intelligent in strategy while others are more intelligent in production. Some of us don't think we can have access to good things, while others would accept nothing less. But all of these factors are variables. On a global scale, foreign currencies are futile, and global markets are based upon constantly changing trends. The value of gold, oil, and cars is becoming less important than air, water, and land in this climate-changing society. Possessions, too, do not define us but are simply another variable adding to our human experience.

I hope you're getting it now. Your identity is the thing about you that will never change, *no matter what* is added or taken away from you. It's the intrinsic part of you that makes you valuable and worthy. You are who you are because a unique set of DNA was put together to add value to the world. Whether you end up a bum on the street or a princess in a palace, you are still *you*.

Isaiah 61:6-9 reminds us of how God sees us. It speaks not only to our own identities being restored, but also that of the generations to come:

> *And you will be called priests of the Lord,*
> *you will be named ministers of our God.*
> *You will feed on the wealth of nations,*
> *and in their riches you will boast.*

> *Instead of your shame*
> *you will receive a double portion,*
> *and instead of disgrace*
> *you will rejoice in your inheritance.*
> *And so you will inherit*
> *a double portion in your land,*
> *and everlasting joy will be yours.*
> *For I, the Lord, love justice;*
> *I hate robbery and wrongdoing.*
> *In my faithfulness I will reward my people*
> *and make an everlasting covenant with them.*
> *Their descendants will be known among the nations*
> *and their offspring among the peoples.*
> *All who see them will acknowledge*
> *that they are a people the Lord has blessed.*

Blessed. Loved. Honoured. Special. Chosen. Seen. Heard. Known. This is who you are; this is how God defined you before you were even born. The weeds don't define you; He does. Find out what it is that is unique about you and wear it like a crown—a crown of beauty, instead of ashes.

 YOUR INVITATION INTO THE GARDEN

When: did you feel like you were being choked by certain people or circumstances in your life?

Where: did you feel like you grew through that experience or became sweeter because of it?

What: can you do this week to change the way you see the situations that God is using to grow you? Or what can you change in order to eliminate a toxic weed from affecting your life?

CHAPTER FIVE

The Water

Restoring Soul

For more than a year, we had drought in Ethiopia. As the water level in the dams got lower and lower, local councils responded by restricting the supply of water to the houses so people would have to go to a pump. We would send a local person to stand in the long lines of people with massive cans, waiting to fill their containers to take back home. Some friends of ours were looking to start a business in an area in Southern Ethiopia that had not had water for a hundred and twenty years. In that region, dust blew into the houses, caking the blankets and belongings with dirt. The local people walked three hours to get water from the closest well. So, when our friends decided to start a cattle-feeding farm in that region, the first thing they did was to dig a well. The day the water was launched was a day of great celebration. People brought their donkeys, their blankets, and clothes they had not washed in a very long time. "We're people too!" they said! They had been forgotten for so long, but now someone had come and given them water.

WATER IS ONE OF THE THREE NECESSARY components for a seed to sprout. Without water, the nutrients that lie within the soil aren't able to be transported into the plant to give it life and help it grow. However, water must be provided in proportionate amounts so the seed isn't flooded out of the very soil it is meant to take root in.

My own story is one of feeling both 'flooded' by turbulent waters and utterly parched, deprived of the life-giving nature of water.

I didn't know what happened within the hospital grounds my father resided in, but I knew that it bore two feelings in me: relief and disdain. Relief because he wasn't at home any more, and disdain because he couldn't be 'normal.' The repercussions of his illness set us apart from our peers at the private Catholic Girl's High School my sisters and I attended. I craved normality. I wanted a father capable of holding down a job and of raising his children. Innately he was a driven hard-worker who desired to provide for his family, but his illness kept him from achieving those goals. His trauma became ours.

My initial response to trauma was flight. Jumping out of windows soon turned into sneaky bus trips into the city where my sister and I would spend hours on end. I found comfort in hiding out. I was trying to escape from the tumultuous waters raging within my soul. Then, after years of feeling like all I could do was leave the room, courage and tenacity began to rise up within me in response to the injustices I felt I had suffered. And so, I fought. I discovered that even though I couldn't fight my father physically, I could fight verbally. I had begun to see the patterns surrounding his mental health, and I used these insights to attack my father's weak spots, playing on his insecurities and brokenness, calling him names, and withholding affection from him in the same way he had withheld it from me. In the midst of the fights, I made a vow to never let him see me cry. The rift between us got wider.

One of my greatest battles with trauma was the temptation to externalise the pain I felt internally. Psychological and emotional abuse leaves a drought within our soul that increases our levels of anxiety and depression. Like the cracks in the ground that eventuate when dirt isn't watered, these two elements indicate a deficiency in our soul.

When I was a teenager, I couldn't stand the pain of unrequited love, and if leaving the room wasn't possible, leaving this life seemed like the next best option. I often thought about how I could take my life, but I feared death. So instead, I took a blade to my wrist and to my hands; I wanted—needed—the pain to shift from the inside to the outside. My heart was thirsting for a love that could quench my drought-stricken soul.

This became my goal in life—to quench my thirst—especially after my parents separated when I was fourteen. The path was laid for all that was broken and cracked in my soul to look for satisfaction in substitutionary liquid.

SATISFIED BY LIVING WATER

In my thirst, I looked to all sorts of things. Drinking alcohol satisfied my drought of confidence and gave me the confidence to speak to people without the inhibitions that came with my low self-esteem and self-loathing, while boys satisfied my thirst to be noticed. Hip-Hop music quenched my soul's desire to connect with people who understood what I was going through, and night clubbing provided a place to dance and find freedom in the midst of people. Yet none of the satisfaction these things offered flowed deep enough; they provided a surface, temporary fix that only left me more parched.

Then in my second to last year of High School, I embarked on a journey to the other side of Auckland as part of a national cultural exchange program. For a few months I found myself surrounded by young people who were ethnically similar to me, yet culturally worlds apart. I had been brought up around Caucasian 'Kiwis' who were middle class home owners—this exchange gave me the opportunity to live in a suburb where Pacific Islanders worked in factories and lived in government housing. Living with a family who were of Samoan heritage, I finally learned more of my mother's cultural background. But rather than feeling like I belonged, I felt even more disillusioned—I had expected to be welcomed as one of their own, but my mixed blood disqualified me from becoming a member of their community. I fit into the category of a 'half caste.'

Although I was staying only thirty minutes away from my home, in the three months that I lived in South Auckland, I realised our families were worlds apart. When I returned home, I struggled to fit back in to where I had come from. Reverse culture shock was not something I had anticipated and neither had the organisers of the program, but it had a greater effect on me than I realised at the time.

The following summer, I spent a lot of time in South Auckland at my aunty's house. My nana was on her death bed at the time, and turns were being taken to nurse her and keep her company as she suffered through her last days of dementia and pneumonia. Being there to witness her last breaths changed the trajectory of my life forever. I no longer had the desire to go back to school or live on the North Shore, and I made the decision to move in with my family 'out South.'

This became a pivotal time for me. The cousin I shared a room with was much more passionate about her faith than I was, but I went with her to the youth group at their local Catholic Church. There I found a community that welcomed me with open arms. They also opened up the Word of God for me and helped me to find direction from it. Within that group setting, my heart started to yearn for change. One of the leaders really took me under her wing and gave me a Bible that I kept beside my bed at night. One night, in the quietness of my room when I was questioning my life's choices up until that point, and recognising I was still thirsty for something more, I opened up my Bible to a page in the middle that contained these words:

> *Take delight in the Lord and he will give you*
> *the desires of your heart.*
>
> Psalm 37:4

I had plenty of desires within my heart that weren't being fulfilled with the lifestyle I had adopted by the age of sixteen. I had quickly learned that while those activities provided me with some temporary happiness, their effects demoralised me. Now, the desire to find my happiness in the things of God began to override the desire to party and drink.

I had started attending a course run by my aunty and uncle aimed at helping high school drop-outs. About a month later, a new guy joined, along with his friend. One day he shared a devotion, speaking on some verses from 1 Corinthians 13, otherwise known as 'the love Chapter.' Immediately I was attracted to his charm as he appealed to the empty void in my soul. Soon after disclosing my secret crush to a mutual friend, he decided to ask me out. It was a day marked by grace: the fifth day of the fifth month, 1995 (five is the number for grace). Little did I know how grace would be introduced to me and carry me through the twenty-one years I would spend in this relationship.

As teenagers, we attended Friday youth nights at the local independent Baptist church where he had first been involved in an after-school kids' program. Afterwards, we would often go out drinking and partying together; even so, it was there that I first heard a gospel of grace and not of works. It was the passion of this young man that I saw exemplified in the walls of the church that kept me going even during the times in our relationship where he would portray addictive, abusive behaviours, much like those that he was surrounded by at home.

Of course, I approached our relationship full of expectations of what I wanted him to be—things he didn't even know I expected of him. Quickly we jumped into a physical, co-dependent relationship, each trying to satisfy our own desires. Our relationship came out of two broken people searching for a watering of their souls. He didn't have the capacity to love me the way I needed to be loved, and my motivation in staying in the relationship, even though I knew it was painful and often cruel, was my innate need to be needed. I also undervalued my beauty and didn't think anyone else would want me. He often affirmed the lies I already believed.

In her book "*Women Who Love Too Much*," Robin Norwood talks extensively about the misconception that people often have toward victimised women who find themselves going from one abusive relationship to another. The misconception is that they are drawn to the pattern of abuse, when in reality, the attraction is actually toward something else. She writes:

> "*When our childhood experiences are particularly painful, we are often unconsciously compelled to recreate similar situations throughout our lives, in a drive to gain mastery over them. For instance, if we . . . loved and needed a parent who did not respond to us, we often become involved with a similar person, or a series of them, in adulthood in an attempt to 'win' the old struggle to be loved.*"

At some point in our relationship, my eighteen-year-old mind conjured up the idea that getting pregnant would have a two-fold benefit. Firstly, we would have to get married. *We could never get married under any other circumstances,* I thought. Secondly, he would have to change—I would have to stop drinking for the sake of the baby, and he would have to stop drinking to support me. Unconsciously, I was forging plans to 'win' this old struggle to be loved and not abandoned.

By this point his drinking problem, which reflected that of his father, was an obvious addiction. Driving past a liquor store required a stop to buy a dozen bottles of beer, and with every stop the aching feeling in my soul grew. I knew this wasn't going to end well; I was thirsting for something else—and it wasn't a commodity from the liquor store.

I wanted a baby, but more than that, I wanted a better life. So, at eighteen, I fell pregnant. We had known each other for just eighteen months. I realised during the pregnancy that addictions and tension would not cease as a result of this life being born. Something deeper needed to happen for change to occur. Though I knew it was not the answer to my real need, as my belly grew and the life within me presented itself to the world, I suggested we should get married.

An Iraqi woman stitched my wedding dress to accommodate my changing body—changes that not only made space for the baby, but also created an openness in me for a new way of life. We continued to attend youth services on Friday nights, only now the messages started to make sense to me in a fresh way. The impending responsibility of raising a child awoke me to the necessity of change.

Change first came two and a half months after we married when our baby was born. Both occasions brought extreme joy into my life. I was elated as I lay beside this man who had just made a commitment to give his life to love me, and held our hairy, dark-skinned boy to my chest. His beautiful entrance into the world brought such sweet hope for our future.

Up to that point, nothing in my life had caused me to marvel at the brilliance of creation like this baby did. One act had led to the development of a human life inside my body, and I was astounded. I held him in my arms, compelled to be grateful to the One who created my new-found love. I couldn't take my eyes off him; he had opened a room in my heart that extended my capacity to love in new ways.

But it was on the nineteenth of October, as we sat in a church full of people, listening to a visiting pastor preach from John chapter four, when what I *knew* finally started to form what I *believed*. Sitting between my sixteen-year-old sister who was eight months pregnant and my mother who was single and in her early forties, I heard for the first time about the woman who met Jesus at the well of Jacob. Jesus knew that this woman had five husbands and lived out of wedlock with the current man she lived with. Yet, in spite of His knowledge of her shameful lifestyle, He (God-incarnate) wanted a relationship with her. He actually wanted to be her friend, and He offered her *living water,* a water that would never make her thirst again.

> *Jesus answered, 'Everyone who drinks this water will be thirsty again, but whoever drinks the water I give them will never thirst. Indeed, the water I give them will become in them a spring of water welling up to eternal life.'*
>
> John 4:13-14

There I was, feeling exposed as the story and shame of a woman who had lived two thousand years before my time, resonated with my own. I, too, was thirsty. I had tried to quench that thirst with attention from the opposite sex, with binge-drinking, and night clubbing—I had even sought religion and behavioural changes, but through a dream, God spoke to me that none of these would ever be enough to meet my need. I was ready for His living water to occupy my soul.

I knew an unseen battle was unfolding as winds rushed through the church building and the banging windows overhead tried to distract me from this eternal offer. I nudged my sister, suggesting she respond, when I realised that the offer wasn't just for her, but for me also. I had spent so much time trying to change those around me, but I had not taken the time to change first. I stepped past my family as tears started to well up in my eyes; my heart was breaking open to make way for the new thing I was about to receive. I pressed against all the resistance that was going on in my mind and walked down the aisle of the church.

That day, I didn't walk a wedding procession of flesh and blood, but of spirit, as Christ took me into His arms to become His bride. As God brought beauty to the ashes of my soul, Isaiah's cries became my own:

> *I am overwhelmed with joy in the Lord my God!*
> *For he has dressed me with the clothing of salvation*
> *and draped me in a robe of righteousness.*
> *I am like a bridegroom dressed for his wedding*
> *or a bride with her jewels.*
>
> Isaiah 61:10, NLT

That day, I confessed my need for Him and my belief that He was risen and alive to set me free. In that moment, my thirst was quenched. Something in my spirit was awakened or 'activated' as I broke open the shell that surrounded my heart to the Sun that desired to show itself more fully to me. My parched roots soaked up the living water, and love was poured into the tips of my very being. I went home that day knowing something had changed.

A NEW CREATION

In the Bible, there are letters written to the New Testament believers who, like me, were struggling to understand the new changes they were going through. Paul, their spiritual father, described what was going on in their heart by using the analogy of circumcision, something that would have been familiar to them. It was an extra layer of flesh that needed to be cut off —just as the shell that surrounds the bud of our heart needs to be removed.

In the Old Testament, circumcision was a picture of the covenant God made with the Jews. By having that layer of flesh cut off, they were signifying they were in relationship with God. Now, under the New Covenant, that picture had been transposed onto the canvas of their heart, whereby Jesus would come and cut away all that separated them from being in relationship with Him, by nailing their sin to the cross. The tragedy of that new way of creating covenant however, is that with their heart, the pain of the cutting didn't have to be experienced by them—it was fully taken on by Jesus. When we burst open the layers that surround our heart to make way for Jesus, even when we don't understand it fully or see it visually, He awakens us by taking the death sentence caused by Adam in the garden, *on Himself*. Jesus came to restore all that was lost in the Garden so that they and we, could become holistically restored and revived. So Paul writes:

> *When you were dead in your sins and in the uncircumcision of your flesh, God made you alive with Christ. He forgave us all our sins, having cancelled the charge of our legal indebtedness, which stood against us and condemned us; He has taken it away, nailing it to the cross.*
>
> Colossians 2:13-14

The symbol of the cross was a prominent feature in my Catholic upbringing, but it wasn't until I understood this truth, that the charges against me had been cancelled, that I was able to live in the full freedom Jesus came to give. He had made me clean. He had made me whole, and now I was His.

Restored, I was ready to go deeper.

DEEP CALLS TO DEEP

Waterfalls are spectacular to observe. As the river drops into the plunge pool below, it impacts the rock face that lies beneath its flow. Deep pools of water are often created at the bottom of the fall, formed by years of relentless pressure as water pounds against the rocks. Growing up in New Zealand, our school camps often took us to places near waterfalls, where I got to observe their beauty and their power firsthand as we swam in the pools they had created.

Personally, I had long known the destructive power of water pressure and the damage that the heavy, over-bearing waters of abuse can inflict as they drop down into the core of our being. Such waters break our sense of security and erode the parts of us that make us feel whole and solid; it can often feel like they chip away aspects of us that we need to keep. But as Christ restored me, I discovered there is another side to waterfalls revealed to us by the psalmist:

> *Deep calls to deep in the roar of Your waterfalls; all Your waves and breakers have swept over me.*
>
> Psalm 42:7

The deep wells where our hearts have become eroded are often the places where God invites us to go deeper with Him; where He invites us to allow the waves and breakers of His love to crash over us. In these places, we must let our deep brokenness meet His deep love for us, for in the depths of our souls, we are crying out for something more—for the garden experience we were created for. And God wants to restore it to us.

After I gave my life to Christ, the greatest enemies to me living as the new creation I now was, were the thoughts that came into my mind, continually exposing the deep wells that existed in my heart. They tried to keep me feeling unworthy by telling me I wasn't good enough and making me doubt that I could do what God had called me to do. I learned that at such times, I needed to dive deeper into God's Word and presence so the depth and wealth of His love and revelation could fill these spaces.

The Bible talks about Jesus loving the Church (His bride) so much that He "gave himself up for her to make her holy, cleansing her by the washing with water through the word . . ." (Ephesians 5:25-26). The

Word of God cleanses us and makes us whole. And while His Word is a gentle cleanser and not a harsh scrub (even if it sometimes feels like it!), it is also imbued with transformative power.

Paul tells us that as we are transformed by the renewing of our mind, we will be able to test and approve what God's will is—His good, pleasing and perfect will (Romans 12:2). As deep as the waters may dig pools into our souls, is the measure of how deep we need to dig into the Word of God to bring truth to the situations we face. In this way, "deep calling out to deep" is fulfilled as alignments are made between the two.

What I love about waterfalls is that they produce a sound so loud in the atmosphere, it's unrelenting. The bigger the waterfall, the greater the noise. And what I have found over the years is that when the lies of the enemy, or the words of an abuser, try to dictate the mood of my day or the direction of my mind, the Word of God is the voice I need to realign me. The depths of your soul can only be comforted by something as deep as His Word. Going to God's Word and allowing the truth to speak into your day, your situation, your life, creates a sound, like the sound of a waterfall, that overrides the other voices you may hear.

God is love, and so, His voice is a voice of love. Love roars like a waterfall out of His heart, and as we access the words He has for us, our mind is renewed and our soul is restored.

 YOUR INVITATION INTO THE GARDEN

When: *did you try to quench your thirsty soul with a substitute that didn't satisfy?*

Where: *was God offering you living water when your supply had run out?*

What: *can you do to increase the volume of truth in your life? How will you drown out the lies of the enemy in your day-to-day experience?*

CHAPTER SIX

The Sprouting

Restoring Calling

In Ethiopia I had a South African friend who loved to grow her own food for her family. We would often pick herbs from outside her kitchen window to use in the cooking we would do together. But it was out the back, in her greenhouse, where my friend prepared and sprouted her seedlings. Taking seedling trays, she would fill them with dirt or water, then plant all kinds of tiny vegetable seeds—kale, beans, tomatoes, broccoli. My friend would move them along the length of the greenhouse, repotting them and tending to them as they matured in this controlled, protected environment, until eventually, they were ready to be picked and eaten.

SPROUTING IS THE TRANSITION between who we used to be and who we're meant to be. It's when we finally break through the shell of all that has held us together and we become undone. In the undoing process, we have the freedom to finally express all that's been going on deep down inside of us so that we can accommodate change. This change from one state to another often becomes uncomfortable to all of those who knew what we were like. There comes a 'kickback' from some about this new image that is being formed in us. It's not familiar to them, and it challenges them about the role they have depended on us to play to keep them in the state that they are in. The sprouting stage in our life will determine the strength of our character and the authenticity of our relationships, while revealing whether we have the resilience to break through the shell that's been holding us 'together' for so long.

'Holding it all together' is what 'religion' does to us. Religion is all about the image and behaviour rather than the heart; about the process and procedure rather than the person; about the law and rules rather than the relationship. Jesus came for the latter and not for the former. He actually came to undo us so that He could draw out of us the beauty we hold within—because all that is beautiful is founded in Him. The undoing is the process of taking down the planks that hold together the planter box that inhibits our growth while giving us a sense of safety and stability.

Some of us don't get to experience the full potential of what God has for us because we are not willing to let ourselves be seen with our cracks and gaps. This takes vulnerability and humility. What our cracks expose, however, is the humanity Jesus came to redeem. Religion often becomes the barrier to us becoming this vulnerable. Religion forges environments that hinder the full expression of who God means us to be as we try to keep our outer layers intact. Unable to find the full expression of who we are (our identity), we busy ourselves with portraying an image of who we think we should be. As a result, however, we end up living behind an inhibiting façade of self-righteousness.

When our sense of obligation to an image or an ideal takes priority over the obligation we have to cultivate our true calling, we get lost in a pursuit that leads us down a path to where we might never fully know who we are. The Bible tells us time and again not to make idols or set up images for ourselves (Leviticus 26:1). We need to take care that we are not making an idol of ourselves, setting ourselves up as an image or façade and bowing down to ourselves rather than to the God who created us. God is all about restoring *His* image in us, for in that place, we find freedom. In contrast, religiousness quenches the Holy Spirit who exists to bring us into that freedom (2 Corinthians 3:17), and it's something that Jesus rebuked:

> *Woe to you, teachers of the law and Pharisees, you hypocrites! You are like whitewashed tombs, which look beautiful on the outside but on the inside are full of the bones of the dead and everything unclean. In the same way, on the outside you appear to people as righteous but on the inside you are full of hypocrisy and wickedness.*
>
> Matthew 23:27-28

When I met Jesus by the well that day (figuratively of course; literally I was in the church), my faith journey took on a new reality but I still felt like I had to hold it all together. This was partly due to a fear of rejection, as my own perception of what was acceptable in church dominated my behavioural patterns. Subtle traces of religion that I thought I had left behind in my traditional and liturgical past were being kept in place by implicit messages about what behaviour was permissible whether inside or outside of church.

THE NEED FOR SELF-AWARENESS

When the prophet Isaiah encountered God, his response went like this:

> *"Woe to me!" I cried. "I am ruined! For I am a man of unclean lips, and I live among a people of unclean lips, and my eyes have seen the King, the Lord Almighty."*
>
> Isaiah 6:5

His response to seeing God and His angels was one of humility; He was undone and became self-aware. Self-awareness is something that is often overlooked in our pursuit of a deeper spiritual connection—but understanding who we are, what we are like, and why we do what we do, are all key elements in healing and restoration.

A seed cannot germinate until it has all the required elements around it to sprout. Water, sun and the right environment will break open the shell of the seed in such a way that a plant is birthed in the breaking. Sometimes in our lives, the elements all seem to be there for that awaited promise in our life to arise. But even when we see nothing with our physical eyes, we can be sure that God is always working to break down our walls so that our mind and heart are ready to enter into our promise.

Isaiah's humility and awareness of both who he was and who God was, propelled him into his calling and purpose—it brought breakthrough.

> *Then one of the seraphim flew to me with a live coal in his hand, which he had taken with tongs from the altar. With it he touched my mouth and said, 'See, this has touched your lips; your guilt is taken away and your sin atoned for.' Then I heard the voice of the Lord saying, 'Whom shall I send? And who will go for us?' And I said, 'Here am I. Send me!'*
>
> Isaiah 6:6-8

When I gave my life to Jesus, He forgave me of my sin and then promptly reminded me of the declaration I made as a child that I would go to a nation far away. One night while feeding my baby boy, I told my husband of my desire to 'one day' go to Ethiopia as a missionary. His response was surprisingly positive. "One day," he said "when the kids are grown up and have moved out." That sat just fine with me—God had given me a new mission field in the area of my home city that had captured my heart during my cultural exchange just a couple of years earlier.

DISCOVERING OUR DEEP GLADNESS

In his book, *Wishful Thinking*, Frederick Buechner writes,

> *[Vocation] comes from the Latin 'vocare', 'to call,' and means the work a man is called to by God. There are all different kinds of voices calling you to all different kinds of work, and the problem is to find out which is the voice of God rather than of Society, say, or the Super-ego, or Self-interest . . . Neither the hairy shirt nor the soft berth will do. The place God calls you to is the place where your deep gladness and the world's deep hunger meet.*

My deepest gladness comes from bringing solutions that assist people in achieving their dreams and outworking their fullest potential. As a six-year-old girl, it seemed like the world's deep hunger existed half way across the world, but then as a sixteen-year-old, I discovered that it existed just across my city.

In Acts 1:8, when Jesus was about to ascend into heaven after His resurrection, He gave His disciples these final instructions:

> *But you will receive power when the Holy Spirit comes on you; and you will be my witnesses in Jerusalem, and in all Judea and Samaria, and to the ends of the earth.*

This progression from Jerusalem to Judea, Samaria, and then to the end of the earth, is a model we can learn from. From their local town, to their region, then to the neighbouring region and then beyond—these are the steps we often have to take to get to where God wants us to go. It's not that any one of those communities is more important than the others, but the experiences you gain along the way build your capacity for what you need to do at whatever "ends of the earth" God is eventually calling you to.

For me, South Auckland became my 'Jerusalem'. Deep needs existed in South Auckland, and I took deep joy in helping to meet those needs. Children lined the streets of this community, and they were all longing to be part of something bigger than their experiences at home. This created a prime opportunity for our church to reach out and bring them into our programs on Sunday mornings and weekday afternoons. As my mum saw me heavily involved in ministry, she reflected on the desire of my heart to be a missionary.

"This is your new mission field isn't it, Michelle?"

"Yeah, it is Mum," I replied.

It was only later in my life that I realised my mum had been the one to first set the example of reaching out to our local community, opening our garage door on frequent occasions and inviting children from the community to do 'Sunday School' right beside our home. She had built a bridge from the community to the church, and now I desired to do the same.

I loved my work in South Auckland, but a few years and four children later, we felt a calling to serve at a local church about three hours' drive from our home city of Auckland. This was my 'Judea.' Talks had already begun about the possibility of us going to Ethiopia in the long term, but for now, the town of Rotorua seemed like a safe first step out of our comfort zone. I used to always hear preachers say, "If you're not ready to go to your next-door neighbour, you're not ready to go on mission across the world." Living in Rotorua helped me to make sense of that.

* * *

Proverbs 27:10 says, "Better a neighbor nearby than a relative far away," and that became true for us during our years in Rotorua where our beautiful elderly neighbours soon became like family to us. They had a garden that ran down their long back yard and extended into a creek. It produced so much vegetation that we often had boxes of their excess waiting at our door when we got home. While family would be our default emergency contacts in Auckland, they were too far away when the battery in the car went flat or I needed someone to watch out for the courier to arrive. Having the courage to build relationships with our next-door neighbours became a habit that would save us from feeling isolated wherever we lived.

We had fewer commitments outside the home in Rotorua, so I signed up for a course where I learned how to prepare a business plan. This awakened in me a passion to plan like I had never experienced before. Coupled with a bible study we were doing at that time called *The Dream Giver*, I started to piece together a formula for how I could connect the church with the community on a larger scale.

> *And the Lord answered me: 'Write the vision;*
> *make it plain on tablets, so that he may run who reads*
> *it. For still the vision awaits its appointed time; it hastens*
> *to the end-it will not lie. If it seems slow, wait for it; it*
> *will surely come; it will not delay.'*
>
> Habakkuk 2:2-3, ESV

I had laid out a plan for downtown Rotorua, but the vision was delayed when a breakdown occurred in our relationship with the people we had moved to Rotorua to help. We moved back to Auckland intending to start making our way to Ethiopia. But soon after we made plans for our return, there was a killing in the neighbourhood where we rented out our home. Suddenly, the vision that I had spent months working on for Rotorua was able to be transplanted into South Auckland to meet the needs there. I rallied support and many people jumped on board. This new venture would take me from being a stay-at-home mum, to being a fully-fledged member of the community in a few short months. My vision to start a youth organisation that would connect the church with the community started to flesh out and sprout much faster than I anticipated. Funds, meetings and programs all started to overwhelm me.

As each new situation presented itself to me, a new opportunity arose to build a foundation for the future calling God had on my life. It is not often that we see how important each opportunity is when we are in the midst of the process. Usually we only see in hindsight how God specifically allowed us to go through a certain experience to prepare us for what lay ahead. That's why the bible encourages us to "not despise these small beginnings, for the Lord rejoices to see the work begin" (Zechariah 4:10, NLT).

If you are carrying a vision that is yet to be outworked, be encouraged today that the seed will break forth! There is value in this time of 'undoing'; as you embrace the sprouting process, you can be sure there will be a gradual unfurling of growth.

 YOUR INVITATION INTO THE GARDEN

When: *have you felt like you have set up an image of yourself that you wanted to portray to the world but knew it wasn't authentic?*

Where: *do you find yourself feeling closed in and not fully allowed to sprout into all that God has called you to be?*

What: *can you do to allow the Holy Spirit to 'undo' you so that you can find true freedom? What do you need to let go of?*

CHAPTER SEVEN

The Branches

Restoring Community

We arrived as a family in Ethiopia the week of their New Year's celebrations. Not knowing that it was tradition to light bonfires to welcome the new year, we were surprised when, one afternoon, people started piling up massive branches inside the gate of our compound and proceeded to light a fire that towered high above our heads. The principal of the school we had come to serve in had arranged the whole thing for us—not only would we have a bonfire like the locals, but we would also be introduced to our first traditional 'coffee ceremony'. "This is to welcome you," he said, "and to introduce you to Ethiopian New Years' Eve culture!" That night, as our two families stood around the fire roasting maize and potatoes, he read us the words of Genesis 12. "Like Abraham," he said, "you have left your home in obedience to God not knowing what lies ahead. But you can be sure that God will bless those who bless you and curse those who curse you."

THE BRANCHES THAT TOWERED ABOVE ME THAT night had been cut for a purpose—to 'graft us in' with the other families that had come to Ethiopia and unite us with what God was doing in our new land.

'Grafting in' is the process where a cut-off branch is placed into the vine of a host tree of the same species. The vine becomes the critical life source for these branches, and because of their connection to the vine, branches which alone would no longer continue to survive, are able to access the nutrients they need to continue growing and bear fruit. Although the fruit may vary from branch to branch, what unites them is that they each grow out of, and are sustained by, their bonding to the host plant which has become its parent, the vine. The unique value and beauty of the fruit born from each graft, makes the host plant more attractive and pleasing than anything else in the garden.

In John 15, Jesus compared our own relationship to Him with this process of being grafted in:

> *I am the vine; you are the branches. If you remain in me and I in you, you will bear much fruit; apart from me you can do nothing.*
>
> John 15:5

Jesus is the Vine and we are the branches, and as we are grafted in—as we abide and remain in Him—we are able to reproduce fruit of His kind; the fruit of the Spirit. But just like a tree doesn't instantly yield fruit, we have to remember that our own ability to bear fruit takes time. It is a gradual process for all the elements of a branch to merge with the Vine, and it is only when this merging is complete that the tree begins to be fruitful. If you've ever had a fruit tree in your garden, you will know it's not always in the first year that you achieve the desired crop—in fact, it can take years before the fruit is as sweet, ripe, and big as you want it to be!

As we wait for our lives to bear the fruit we want it to, we have to trust that change will happen, and that we are living for a God who is far more patient with us than we are with Him. He's the God who created seasons like spring and fall. He doesn't expect full-fledged fruit to be available immediately, so why do we expect it for ourselves? He doesn't pull away when we're still getting assimilated in; that's why He calls us to draw closer and just stay—to "not become weary in doing good, for at the proper time we will reap a harvest if we do not give up" (Galatians 6:9).

LONGING FOR FRUITFULNESS

After I was first grafted into the Vine, I became immersed in the life of our church. The lifestyle of our family changed—we started serving in children's programs at church and I enrolled myself in Bible College studies to gain a better understanding of this 'book' that had finally started to make sense in my life. But not all the changes came easily or readily; I found it simpler to give up things like smoking and drinking compared to conquering wrong thoughts and defeating unforgiveness.

As I dove into my studies, I realised the Bible actually had more to say about these struggles than the former habits I had typically associated with Christianity. Jesus' teaching in Matthew 5:27-28 made me realise that God was more interested in dealing with the heart issues than in me keeping all the rules.

> You have heard that it was said, 'You shall not commit adultery.' But I tell you that anyone who looks at a woman lustfully has already committed adultery with her in his heart.

At that time, my heart rang 'guilty' of the content of this verse. A desire to be loved remained unfulfilled in my heart as the physical, emotional, and spiritual rifts within my marriage grew and I found myself battling to conquer thoughts for someone who wasn't my husband. I didn't want to have these thoughts; I knew they were wrong, so I took it in my own hands to rid myself of them.

I didn't understand it at the time, but these thoughts stemmed from a place of co-dependency—I had found a person who needed to be rescued, and immediately slipped into the role of the rescuer. Old habits started to tempt me again, and without knowing what to do with the internal struggle, my default reaction was to focus on the external issue—my attraction. I confessed my thoughts to my husband, repenting that the affection that should have belonged solely to him was being robbed from the fortress of my mind.

His initial reaction was calm and understanding, but a delayed explosion was about to let me know how he really felt. Confronted with the fact that he himself had been unfaithful during my pregnancy, not just in his mind but in someone else's bed, his anger was momentarily appeased. I, however, became increasingly disillusioned as I realised that what I thought we had sealed in my pregnancy had still not been sanctified in his heart.

This old fruit of insecurity and rejection grew into stubborn, thorn-filled branches, which threatened the grafting process that was taking place. Needing intervention, I called on our pastor and his wife. I gave them permission to speak into our marriage, and by allowing the light to expose our dirt, its effects were made all the more obvious. But I soon realised my husband was happy hiding from reality and content to stay that way.

Around this time, my parents stepped in to help us buy our own home. Here we were, twenty years old with one income and a baby, signing off on a mortgage. From that point on, more often than not, we had people living with us to either help pay the mortgage or because they needed somewhere to stay. I loved hosting people, so I was always happy to make room for them—that, and keeping up appearances was important to both of us—and their presence forced our arguments to be tame, offering me a sense of safety.

We had bought a large family home, and it didn't take long before half of my family had moved in—we soon had my mother, and my younger brother and sister living with us. They were young and impressionable and my strategy to prevent them from ending up like us was to bring them to church. So we got increasingly involved in our church, picking up kids off the street on a Sunday morning whose parents were still recovering from their hangovers from partying the night before. In that community, youth gangs were prevalent and young girls prostituted themselves for two dollars because they thought it was fun. My heart broke for the families that surrounded us. I knew their pain, and I knew the answer to that pain.

My strategy worked to a degree, and my siblings also started to get involved in church life. However, despite being busy with ministry, life at home still carried the burdens we bore before we entered into our new life with Christ. Within our first year of living in our new home, the holes in the wall reflected the frustration that was frequently directed at me. Though this disturbed me, I didn't classify those attacks as abuse because my body wasn't harmed. Yet my mind assuredly was.

At the age of twenty-one, I fell pregnant again. The branches of our family were expanding, but this time, I felt ready to take on the challenge. With my family living with us at the time, I felt like I had enough support around me—until I found out we were pregnant with twins. Having seen my mother struggle with twins fourteen years earlier, I knew this would be hard work, and I struggled to think positively about the responsibility I was carrying. I did, however, after having a boy, look forward to having two baby girls to dress up and hang out with when they were grown women!

My mother moved out of our home during my pregnancy, leaving my brother and sister for us to raise through their teenage years. The support I thought I could rely on was now gone and there I was pregnant with twins, now raising twin teenagers!

The day after my girls were born, my world got turned upside down even further. Overwhelmed and sleep deprived, my husband came to the birthing unit to tell me he had just lost his job. After months of taking advantage of his position, he had resigned and started a new job. However, an investigation was underway and the truth was exposed. He'd been pulled from his new place of work, taken into custody, and charged with theft. I had suspected something was wrong for months, but all I had known was lies. I felt so alone. Once again, I found myself in the midst of a pattern that kept repeating itself: Lies and deception, manipulation and defensiveness, repentance and change. I was always ready to forgive a changed person, yet the cycle continued, and I was frustrated that I was always the one that paid for his actions.

HIDDEN GROWTH

For a branch to be successfully grafted into the trunk of a tree, there has to be a support mechanism that connects the branch onto the trunk until all of its tissues have connected with those of the trunk. A great amount of growing needs to happen internally during this time; growth which is largely unseen to the naked eye. In the same way, we need support around us to help us grow internally in a way that prepares us to be truly connected to the Vine.

It is a misconception that once you become a Christian, your life miraculously changes. It is true that your past is behind you and you can walk forward knowing you are a new person, However, while this is true in our spirit being, in our holistic make-up, the process of salvation is an ongoing journey. 1 Thessalonians 5:23-24 says:

> *May God himself, the God of peace, sanctify you through and through. May your whole spirit, soul and body be kept blameless at the coming of our Lord Jesus Christ. The one who calls you is faithful, and he will do it.*

That word 'sanctify' means to be separate or set apart. Like a branch that's been cut off from one tree and grafted into another, God sets us apart in order to place us into the Vine. He's the Vine who offers a peace that surpasses all understanding, and as we get grafted in to Him, His peace is available to us at our discretion. But as we detach from the world, we need to trust Him enough to attach ourselves fully and holistically to Him. While we desire peace, we must learn to let go of anxiety. When we desire love, we have to let go of hate and co-dependency (which is a counterfeit of love, as it is motivated by selfish intentions). When we desire forgiveness, we have to let go of bitterness and hurt. When we desire physical health, we have to let go of detrimental eating habits and laziness. Jesus desires to give us all of these gifts, but we have to recognise what we are still holding onto—and why.

One of the things that supports this transition process is God's love. Paul tells us:

> *And I pray that you, being rooted and established in love, may have power, together with all the Lord's holy people, to grasp how wide and long and high and deep is the love of Christ, and to know this love that surpasses knowledge – that you may be filled to the measure of all the fullness of God.*
>
> Ephesians 3:17-19

To be filled to the measure of the fullness of God is to know this love that surpasses knowledge. The love God has for us creates security during this time of hidden growth and prepares us for later seasons of external, visible fruitfulness. God is love, He calls us to be ambassadors of His kingdom of love, and to do that we first have to somehow grasp the extent of that love in our minds, letting it sink into our hearts. His love is what we are called to be deeply rooted and established in—and it's only from this place of being grafted into Him that we can truly be filled with the 'full measure' of all that He has so we can then share it with others.

BECOMING CONNECTORS

We live in a disconnected world. More than ever before, loneliness, depression, and insecurity pervade society. People are searching for a place to belong and they are not always open to coming into a church building to find that belonging. We must be the connectors between the community and the church. It sounds a little cliché, but in a world where churches have been closed down for longer periods than ever before, we have *to be* the Church, not just *go* to church, because the hope we have for a better day, is not only for us but for those around us.

The model of 'beauty for ashes' in Isaiah 61 portrays those who have been restored as being planted all over the place in testimony to what God has done.

> *The Sovereign LORD will show his justice to the nations of the world. Everyone will praise him! His righteousness will be like a garden in early spring, with plants springing up everywhere.*
>
> Isaiah 61:11, NLT

God wants to bring social justice and change. He longs to bring balance, equity, and righteousness. This righteousness is not about attaining a certain level of sinlessness, and in this case, it's not even about our behaviour. The Hebrew word translated as righteousness, *tzedaqah,* actually derives from the word *tzedaq* which means justice. In Jewish culture, families often have a *tzedaqah* box where they collect money for those who have little. It is a way of life rather than an ad-hoc donation people give only when they are asked to.

In the same way, righteousness is about making wrong things right. It calls us to be ambassadors of Christ, continuing what was prophesied of Him: "Every valley shall be raised up, every mountain and hill made low; the rough ground shall become level, the rugged places a plain" (Isaiah 40:4). When the mountain is too high for people to climb, and we supply the mechanism to help them to climb it, that is righteousness. When young people are struggling with hopelessness and despair and we show them the road to fulfil their purpose, that is righteousness. When refugees are stuck in our land without knowing how to navigate the social structures that are around them, and we help them, that is righteousness.

That verse, "His righteousness will be like a garden in early spring, with plants springing up everywhere," speaks, I believe, of many charities and social justice organisations arising in places of need, led by God's people. But it also speaks of *us* arising right where we are planted. Often we are more susceptible to the needs of those who are in the midst of situations we too have experienced—this is where the ashes of our personal experiences build a crown of beauty that others can see and be drawn to. It is what I call the 'ministry of acquaintance', where, like Jesus, we become acquainted with the grief of those who are facing similar struggles and circumstances to what we have walked through. It is where we put 2 Corinthians 1:3-5 into action:

> *Praise be to the God and Father of our Lord Jesus Christ, the Father of compassion and the God of all comfort, who comforts us in all our troubles, so that we can comfort those in any trouble with the comfort we ourselves receive from God. For just as we share abundantly in the sufferings of Christ, so also our comfort abounds through Christ.*

While living in South Auckland, I attended a community development workshop with a guest speaker who was well known for the books she had written and her extensive work in the justice system and community. She spoke about how most of the women who had been referred to her organisation had an average of twelve other organisations approaching them with offers of help. This was overwhelming for most families, who often felt lost in the system and disconnected from all of them. Her recommendation was to have one 'gatekeeper' so that the family wasn't constantly bombarded by service providers. The organisation the beneficiary had the strongest relationship with would become their 'gatekeeper' and the one who funnelled communications to them.

This organisational model can inform us as we seek to disciple other believers and support them in their own process of being fully grafted into the body of Christ. In a sense, we are all called to be *someone's* gatekeeper. There is someone out there who needs you to stand in the gap for them, to help them to buffer the many voices that are bombarding them—internally and externally. When someone walks alongside you in your season of need and shares the burden you carry, it eases the load.

> *Brothers and sisters, if someone is caught in a sin, you who live by the Spirit should restore that person gently. But watch yourselves, or you also may be tempted. Carry each other's burdens, and in this way you will fulfil the law of Christ. If anyone thinks they are something when they are not, they deceive themselves.*
>
> Galatians 6:1-3

As you come alongside those who God calls you to support, it's important to remember *it's not about you*. We have to be careful that we don't develop a hero complex. We are simply a conduit of the river of the Holy Spirit—what we have to offer has been deposited into us by an outside resource. It is God alone who is the giver of abundant life, so when we are bringing life and hope to someone else, it is the essence of God flowing through us. The season that they are in will be determined by time, and your involvement in that will be seasonal also. You may develop a friendship over a longer period of time, but we have to watch out that our relationships do not lead to co-dependence, but result in maturity.

James offers a lot of wisdom for when God calls us to be a 'gatekeeper'. He is one of those apostles who tells it like it is! There is no beating around the bush with James. He reminds us that "every good and perfect gift is from above, coming down from the Father of the heavenly lights, who does not change like shifting shadows" (James 1:17).

When we are grafted into Christ, we draw everything we have from Him, the Vine. If we truly understand that without *Him* we can do nothing, then we have the power to release what is in our hands, knowing it is only ours to steward. But when we think we have earned what we have, then we can tend to withhold it from others. This is not the way of God or true religion.

> *Religion that God our Father accepts as pure and faultless is this: to look after orphans and widows in their distress and to keep oneself from being polluted by the world.*
>
> James 1:27

When we play a part in restoring an orphan by being a parent to them, or a widow by providing support, we are displaying the true essence of what God is like, for a "father to the fatherless, a defender of widows, is God in his holy dwelling" (Psalm 68:5).

In Isaiah 61, God has given us a list of those whom He came to restore; namely, the poor, the broken-hearted, the captives, the prisoners, and the blind. And throughout Scripture, He repeatedly calls us to look after the widow, the orphan, and the foreigner, each of whom have some degree of relationship and connection missing in their lives:

A widow: Her husband, soul mate, provider and protector—the closest one.

An orphan: Their parents, their providers, their protectors—the closest two.

A foreigner: Their community, their home, their whole family—the closest few.

God's intention is that we would all experience intimacy in our relationships, that we would know a mother and a father's love, and that we would be a part of a greater family and community. When these elements of our human experience have been lost, He comes in and calls His children to fill the gap. When people are grieving and mourning because they have experienced loss, we can be assured that He is acquainted with their grief.

We all have a part to play in the restorative plan of God. I see a movement of people returning to their first love and seeing God for who He is—a generous God who came to give us a life of abundance so that we can overflow into the lives of others. This was the reality of the early church and He wants it to become ours also. They had just had God in the flesh, living and dwelling among them, and they continued this ministry of 'being God with flesh on.' It is this sort of righteousness that brings equity across communities. In Acts 2:44-45 we read:

> *All the believers were together and had everything in common. They sold property and possessions to give to anyone who had need.*

Those who were in need were looked after in such a way that even outsiders saw the church as a community who loved deeply. Their faith in God caused them to devise a system that ensured everyone was looked after. As I walked the streets of Ethiopia one day, I wondered if the church would ever be reawakened to this kind of living. I had grown up living in a country with a social welfare system that looked after those who were in financial hardship, and now my heart was breaking for those who didn't have that kind of support to rely on. I heard stories of people who had been through seasons where they couldn't find work and were left hungry, homeless, and forced into prostitution out of lack of better options.

Isaiah 9:6 contains the prophesy that "the government will be upon His [Jesus'] shoulder." In my years in Ethiopia, I wondered if we, the church, could be the expression of that government, providing support for those who needed to get through a rough season—not to disempower them, but to carry them through the transition from one season to another and to enable them to become fully grafted in to the Vine. Will you be a part of His government? Will you extend your branches to provide them shade when they need it?

🌿 YOUR INVITATION INTO THE GARDEN

When: *did you understand that you were a part of something bigger than yourself?*

Where: *do you feel like God is calling you into a community? How do you think you can be a stream of income, influence, or encouragement to them?*

What: *can you do to improve the lives of others? What are you so aware of because of your own experience, that you could advocate for?*

CHAPTER EIGHT

The Roots

Restoring Hearts

Zion Church, where I served as a Sunday School teacher, minister of the Word and English service pastor, had five outreach churches in rural Ethiopia. It was dry season when I was asked to go and preach at one of those churches. I sat in the front cabin between the driver and my pastor's wife, Nigist, when my eyes were drawn to a massive Acacia tree in the middle of the field. This was a typical African, lion-king-style tree with big chunky, spreading roots that were so old they had risen above the ground. That's the wonder of maturity. In the dry season, nothing else was growing. But this tree had grown to the point where even in a dry season its roots were able to source enough water from the ground to sustain it.

Our roots often reveal issues that need to be dealt with before we can grow and mature. When we carry unresolved trauma and abuse, or walk with unforgiveness, holding on to offences, we often struggle to trust not only other people, but also God. When we don't understand that God is fully trustworthy, we forfeit our ability to be transparent with Him about the pain and hurt we feel. And when we can't trust Him with our pain, we prevent our roots from going down deep and drawing from His water. God taught me this lesson when one of my evening runs ended with a mishap.

That night I wanted to cover a good distance without stopping (as frequent stops had become a part of my routine in re-building my fitness). Proud of my achievement, I'd gone further than normal, and when I turned around an unfamiliar corner my toe stubbed against an uneven pavement block and I fell forward. I was holding my phone in my hand, and used that hand to break the fall, scratching up both my phone and my hand. I called my mum to pick me up, and when I got home and looked at my knee, I discovered an ugly scrape. I spent a week nursing my wounds so they wouldn't get infected, but just over a week later, although my hand was almost fully healed, my knee still looked nasty. The difference between the two was that I had left my hand exposed, carefully tending to it throughout the week, while my knee had been covered up by long pants and dresses—not just because the weather was cold, but so that people wouldn't get grossed out when they saw how scabby it was.

We do the same with our wounded hearts. We think that if we just cover up the wounds, they will eventually heal themselves and we won't have to worry about people seeing how ugly they look. Exposure requires vulnerability, and vulnerability requires humility. Vulnerability is hard for most people. It takes a level of trust that goes beyond human comprehension, yet it brings human connection at levels that can't be explored otherwise. The only way we can find complete healing is by becoming vulnerable and exposing the ugliness of what we endured—the pain we suffered or inflicted. In exposing the wounds, we allow the tenderness of empathy to transform that scab into a scar.

Don't be ashamed of your scars. Scars speak of healing and restoration, while wounds speak of unfinished business. We can finish the business of healing our wounds once we vulnerably admit that they exist, expose them to those who know how to properly bring healing to them, and take time to allow for the healing process.

I love what Oswald Chambers wrote in his devotional book, *My Utmost for His Highest*:

> *"Growth in grace is measured not by the fact that you have not gone back, but that you have an insight into where you are spiritually; you have heard God say, 'Come up higher,' not to you personally but to the insight of your character... 'Shall I hide from Abraham that thing which I do?' God has to hide from us what He does until by personal character we get to the place where He can reveal it."*

I knew that God desired to restore me psychologically by repairing the damage that had been done, but at the age of twenty-nine, I was brutally confronted with the fact that I had not yet dealt with my childhood trauma. Amongst the insecurities and rejection that were rooted in my soul, the environment that was being cultivated in my marriage and ministry was setting me up for the biggest fall of my life.

EMBRACING 'GOOD SUFFERING'

We need depth of character able to sustain the growth and fruit our lives will bear. When we address the effects of trauma and sin in our hearts, we build capacity for internal growth. Although we might never fully remove all of the effects of what we have suffered, we can choose to let them *grow us* instead of *slow us*.

Romans 5:1-5 says:

> *Therefore, since we have been justified through faith, we have peace with God through our Lord Jesus Christ, through whom we have gained access by faith into this grace in which we now stand. And we boast in the hope of the glory of God. Not only so, but we also glory in our sufferings, because we know that suffering produces perseverance; perseverance, character; and character, hope. And hope does not put us to shame,* **because God's love has been poured out into our hearts through the Holy Spirit,** *who has been given to us.*

These verses bring a powerful perspective to the often-painful process of healing. The key to our broken hearts being mended and the reason for our hope is this: Our suffering need not be fruitless; it has the ability to produce something beautiful in our lives. This is why we sometimes speak of a 'good kind of suffering.' Addictions are simply our way of trying to avoid suffering. But we need to understand that choosing to ignore the good suffering only brings further suffering. There are consequences to leaving our wounds unhealed.

I experienced the pain of ignoring 'good suffering' firsthand. I was at home with the kids preparing for a marriage retreat, when I received a call from a lady who worked for the organisation we wanted to serve with in Ethiopia. She had looked over our application form and seen that we had experienced infidelity in our marriage. In the sweetest spirit, she suggested that we get counselling before we venture out into international ministry. Her suggestion wasn't a rejection of our application but rather it was being put on hold—they wisely recognised that we needed to take some time to pursue healing.

Setting out with this news fresh on my mind was hard, but I hoped that the retreat would help ease the tension. After my husband and I had dropped the children off for the weekend and began heading out of the city, I informed him of the phone call and let him know that it was his mistake that might cost us time in getting to the land I longed for. We were driving through one of the many gorges that make up the landscape of New Zealand when we came to a standstill because of an accident that had happened further up the road. There we sat, stuck in traffic with this contentious subject hanging in the car like a fuzzy dice on our windscreen. The subject just hung there, and it was starting to irritate us.

What we failed to see in that moment was the lesson being displayed. You see, we were sitting in the middle of the road with no way forward. We could forget the trip and go home, or we could simply turn around for a little while, have a coffee at the nice café at the entrance to the gorge and when the traffic cleared, we could continue on our way. The call from the mission agency was asking us to do the same thing: Turn back for a little while, process what had happened, get to the root causes—the brokenness, the stress reactors that caused this affair to happen— and find healing, and then we could get back on the road to Ethiopia again.

Instead, an internal volcano erupted, pouring hot lava on the soil of our hearts. It reminded me of a region of black rock on our grandparents' island of Samoa where lava once flowed, killing all existing vegetation. Nothing will ever grow through that hardened molten rock because the roots have been burnt out and buried. That's what we so often do with our problems—we burn them and bury them, hoping no one will ever dig them out. But what results is barrenness and dark shadows where light and life desire to be displayed.

That day, we couldn't see beyond the temporary detour we had to make. We didn't want to embrace the 'good suffering', and we were going to suffer regardless. Blame, manipulation, anger and abuse smothered the light that desired to bring life out of our dead situation. We turned what could have been an opportunity for growth into an occasion for the dysfunction of our hearts to rule our decision-making, *again*. My husband felt rejected, and so he rejected the idea of going to Ethiopia. Since there was no going back, we agreed to move forward into endeavours that were opening up for us in New Zealand.

When we don't deal with the root issues in our lives, the bad fruit they produce will always resurface. We can cut off the external expression of those roots and carry on, but eventually, they will grow back. This is what we saw happen over the next year of our lives, as we went out into the community to outwork a vision I had to provide a community centre for at-risk youth. On the outside, we seemed to be doing great things. High profile individuals and organisations supported my vision. Money started flooding in, and we started pouring out all that we had to see this vision come to fruition. But it didn't take long before the roots of our dysfunction broke open the buds of despair. Tension and distrust stemmed from our roots of addiction and insecurity. While our desire was to help young people in the community, the young people in our home (our very own offspring) were being neglected. Life's demands were tipping the scale. I was about to make the biggest mistake of my life.

* * *

It started with a text message from a young man from one of the programs we were running. Could we meet up to talk? As I had listened to his story of brokenness and despair, my own unmet longings surfaced and I believed the lie they told—that this young man wasn't only about to unknowingly fill my void, but that I was about to fill his.

After a big event one night, I dropped my children home, sculled down a glass of wine and, making plans via a text message, met up with him on a residential street where, for the first time since I had first kissed my husband, I kissed another man. Here I was, twenty-nine with five children, a reputation in the community, an organisation under my leadership, and an extended family who looked up to me, caught up in the feelings of a moment. So caught up was I, that I didn't think about the aftermath—how would I return home to my loved ones? How would I face this young man in the future? How would I account for my disappearance for the time away from home? I believed the lie that no-one would ever have to know.

The next morning, I woke to the stark reality of my betrayal. I needed to confess to my husband what I had done—but in the end, I didn't have to. We had an activity planned for that day, taking a van-load of young people to the beach for an outing. It was as I was driving that my husband came across the text message on my phone. In a jealous rage, he began screaming questions at me before throwing his fist at my face. In what I felt was a justified response, I received it. Leaving him with the van full of kids, I got out and headed back home feeling the enormity of what had just transpired.

The consequences of my infidelity and our marital distress reached every part of our lives. The board of trustees I had formed removed me as their chairperson, and our pastor called to tell me he wasn't interested in us taking other people down the road that we were heading. Overnight, it seemed, we had lost our reputation and the respect of those we had led, along with our positions and responsibilities in our own organisation. But above all, we had lost who we were as people. In the grief and turmoil that followed, and feeling like his life was crushed, my husband turned to alcohol once again. Feeling helpless and guilty, I soon joined him in the drama I had been rescued from only a decade earlier. The irony was that, even though it looked like I was lying in a bed I had made for myself, I didn't want to be there. I knew I needed help.

RECEIVING HELP

It is not easy to have our mess and our brokenness exposed, but when we reach out for help, we find we have access to grace and peace through the person of Jesus. As we persevere through the pain of the healing process, we gain character and find hope again for a greater future. The understanding that we're not walking through this process alone is powerful. The very gaps exposed in your soil—the depths of your soul, your very heart—will be filled with the love of God poured out through the Holy Spirit.

In order for our wounds to fully heal, we must once again be willing to revisit the trauma we have experienced in our lives, our 'less-than-the-garden' experiences. Revisiting the 'death' we experienced in those places and then grieving the loss we suffered, leads us into the resurrection of our hearts, enabling us to truly live again. Too many of us allow the traumatic events we have suffered to remain in power. But we have the choice to take back the power over our lives, acknowledge our mistakes, and live in freedom. However, our ability to experience this freedom is contingent on whether or not we will be loyal to our own healing or to those who have inflicted the pain.

The realisation that I needed help, however, brought back memories of my experiences as a teenager waiting in the offices of psychiatric doctors who sat behind clipboards. Compounding these negative associations was the fact that looking to external sources for psychological help wasn't greatly encouraged at our church. This, and a million other excuses, meant we didn't pursue healing in our marriage. It was obvious issues needed to be dealt with, but we were surviving with our dysfunction, so we continued bearing its load.

When someone has grown up in a violent home, it seems absurd that they would continue to choose to accept that as an adult. But although I had counselled many people through similar circumstances, and even attended training for working with abuse victims, I didn't recognise that I was in the same position. Because the abuse wasn't yet named, it was easy to tolerate. In fact, at that point, I just believed I deserved it.

Without no sense of my identity or self-worth, there was a sense that my life was somehow fake. I lived at a surface level, and while I desired to break into new territory, the innate response to defend myself and everything I believed kept me from engaging with my true self. Thankfully, the prophet Jeremiah had some advice for me:

> But blessed are those who trust in the Lord and have made the Lord their hope and confidence. They are like trees planted along a riverbank with roots that reach deep into the water. Such trees are not bothered by the heat or worried by long months of drought. Their leaves stay green, and they never stop producing fruit.
>
> Jeremiah 17:7-8, NLT

I wanted to be like the trees Jeremiah described—I wanted to have roots that reached down deep, drawing on living water, but something was hindering me from doing so. When our roots can't stretch out, it's like coming up against the floor of a flowerpot; we find ourselves hitting rock bottom, and because there's only so much room for growth, life becomes a surface display of beauty, but beneath the surface, there's no depth—no depth of character, intimacy, integrity, or self-worth. Like the verse in Jeremiah demonstrates, where the roots are planted affects how the tree will flourish.

* * *

It would be some years later, when my marriage finally came to an end, that I was given a gift in the form of a beautiful Ethiopian psychotherapist. Meeting up with her for coffee, she told me she had been reading a book about women who find themselves in relationships with addicts and offered to lend it to me. This came as an answer to a prayer I had prayed a few weeks earlier: "Lord, show me what I'm not seeing. If there's something in me, some root that is causing these problems in my marriage, show me!"

As I read, I began to see the co-dependent tendencies I had

developed as a result of my childhood trauma. I had been planted by healing streams—one of which was the book I had just read, and another was my psychotherapist. She became an invaluable resource, taking me through grief counselling and giving me advice as I navigated the separation that would lead to divorce. She also recommended that I attend an Alcoholics Anonymous support group, and this became another source of restorative healing for me.

Slowly I was learning to deconstruct the thoughts that made God seem unapproachable. I had gotten to the point where I thought, *I will never be good enough for God, so why should I even try anymore?* Sometimes, we hide our pain from God because we think He is just out to punish us like our birth fathers might have. But the Word of God flips that belief on its head:

> *For the word of God is alive and active. Sharper than any double-edged sword, it penetrates even to dividing soul and spirit, joints and marrow; it judges the thoughts and attitudes of the heart. Nothing in all creation is hidden from God's sight. Everything is uncovered and laid bare before the eyes of him to whom we must give account. Therefore, since we have a great high priest who has ascended into heaven, Jesus the Son of God, let us hold firmly to the faith we profess. For we do not have a high priest who is unable to empathize with our weaknesses, but we have one who has been tempted in every way, just as we are—yet he did not sin. Let us then approach God's throne of grace with confidence, so that we may receive mercy and find grace to help us in our time of need.*
>
> Hebrews 4:12-16

We never need to be afraid of coming to God or allowing our roots to be exposed! As we approach God's throne of grace, we can come with confidence—even when we have made the biggest mistakes. He already knows what we have done, and He loves us anyway. Only when we understand the extent of His grace and mercy and the impact it can have on us, will we fully receive the restoration He wants to bring. And when our heart is restored, we'll be able to put down those roots; we'll be able to withstand whatever life throws us—whether that be heat or long months of drought—and keep growing as God intended us to.

🌿 YOUR INVITATION INTO THE GARDEN

When: *have you decided to be vulnerable and had it met with empathy?*

Where: *do you see woundedness in your heart, resurfacing in your reactions to triggers?*

What: *is in your life that you need to trust the Lord for as your healer and provider?*

CHAPTER NINE

The Pruning

Restoring Relationship

One of the ministries we were involved with in Ethiopia was called "Hope House." The house was positioned in an area known as Lemlem, meaning 'fertile.' I was excited about the house, but even more so about the roses that grew in the garden. I envisaged it as a wide-open space where our residents would be able to step out into and enjoy the beauty of their Creator. But one morning as I walked through the gates of the compound, I was horrified to discover our guard had chopped all the tops off the branches on the rose bushes. He'd been so severe in his pruning that they looked like they had no hope of ever growing again. Being an amateur gardener, I asked him why he had cut them back so far—he just laughed at me and insisted I trust what he had done would have good results. Of course, it didn't take long before the rose bushes did bloom again. Only this time, what they produced was far more beautiful and bountiful than what they had previously produced. I learned then that my gardener friend knew way better than I did!

It was in Ethiopia that I learned the value of pruning—not only in the case of the rose bushes, but in my own life as well. In John 15, Jesus says:

> *I am the true vine, and my Father is the gardener. He cuts off every branch in me that bears no fruit, while every branch that does bear fruit he prunes so that it will be even more fruitful.*
>
> John 15:1-2

Pruning is painful. It implies some cutting off needs to take place, and let's be honest, cutting never feels good. We require an extra measure of faith in the Gardener during this process.

I had begun working at Hope House, but things were not going well. My oldest son had just returned from New Zealand after eighteen months of being away, and my husband was away working in Southern Ethiopia six days of the week. This left me to both run the project *and* manage our own home with five children—not to mention the constant stream of people visiting from overseas.

Within the compound itself, there was conflict between the staff members. The very people who were meant to be showing unconditional love to those who didn't know what such a love was like, couldn't even show love to one another! The women we were helping were struggling to find work, our finances were looking slim—and to top it off, funds had gone missing. I didn't know who was responsible for the theft, and it undermined my confidence in my team. I was confused about *everything* that was happening in my life but a decision had to be made about the fate of this project, and at that point I made an executive decision to close it down.

I was already on the verge of being burnt out when I got sick with typhoid. This tipped me over the edge. By now, I was done with Ethiopia. I left the country disillusioned, on a four-month break to take our eldest son back home. My prayer was "If you want us to stay, I am willing." I had never thought I would get to that place and yet God allowed me to; He saw my heart and knew the struggle. He had started to make an incision into the branch He would eventually prune from me, but not before He gave me a glimpse of the beautiful lateral shoots that would be produced.

* * *

For pruning to be successful and result in increased growth, it has to be done where there is a 'growth bud' on the branch. There are different types of these buds, but the two we're concerned with are called the 'terminal bud' and the 'lateral bud.' A terminal bud grows at the tip of a shoot and causes the shoot to grow longer. These buds produce hormones that move downward along the shoot, inhibiting the growth of other buds on that shoot. Lateral buds on the other hand, grow along the sides of a shoot and give rise to the sideways growth that makes a plant fuller. These buds stay dormant until the shoot has grown long enough to diminish the influence of the hormones produced by the terminal bud, or until the terminal bud is pruned off; then they begin their growth.

Picture two types of branches—a long branch with a little bud at the top that is sending hormones down its shoot to keep the head strong, and then a shorter branch with buds, that has many branches growing off the side. The first is that way because it has a terminal bud at the top, lengthening the branch by inhibiting other branches from shooting off from its source. The second enables growth on its side once it has become greater in strength than the terminal bud or has had that terminal bud pruned.

It makes little sense for a person to be cut off, (separated or removed) from our lives when they seem to have such a key position in the arrangement that we display to the world. But sometimes those people, no matter how significant, inhibit our growth like the terminal bud. Today's society objectifies the 'happy family' as the nuclear family that stays together through thick and thin. Social pressure (especially amongst Christian families) to stay together even when abuse is occurring, can allow dysfunction to move downward into the next generation, inhibiting their development.

The same could be said of leaders of organisations, ministries, or companies. When their position is inhibiting the growth of those they were called to lead, then they too can become like a terminal bud. The innate desire within us for power and control, means that, when we can't have things our way, our perspective of others can change. We no longer see them as adding value to the whole community, but rather as a hindrance to us having our way. Whenever there is growth that inhibits fruitfulness, there is a need for pruning to occur.

* * *

For us, severe pruning was needed in our family. The image we had displayed started to crack one particular night in New Zealand on the eve of what was meant to be a speaking engagement at our church's Men's Breakfast. I had spoken in churches in Australia and New Zealand already during our time away, and I loved how God spoke to me and through me during those messages. Yet this one event made me question my integrity in sharing at all.

I had spent that day with my family after my nephew had been involved in a near fatal, alcohol-induced car accident in the Pacific Island he was working on. I had been making trips to the airport and back to my sister's house all day, leaving them with the impact of my nephew's injuries still unknown. As I arrived back that night at my in-laws' home, I was confronted by loud music. But the drunken look I saw in my husband's eyes screamed even louder. Perhaps it was a message he had been screaming at me internally for a while, but my ears had become deaf to their plea. That night, alcohol left my husband completely uninhibited. He became abusive and reckless, and emotions escalated on both sides. It was clear we had reached the point where separation was necessary for the safety of our children. It was at this point that I was forced to put out an ultimatum—the drinking stops, or the marriage ends.

* * *

Our family returned to Ethiopia a few months later, and by then, something in me had changed. A new anointing had begun to flow in me, a flow of the Holy Spirit that would set me up to win as we embarked on a new season of ministry in Ethiopia.

On our return, we took up residence in Addis Ababa where we had access to a better school along with a home school community for our children's extra-curricular needs. This school was home to good friends who had supported us through my seasons of confusion and joy, and soon I would need their support more than ever because my husband had decided to return to New Zealand. While the reason he gave was that he wanted to take up studies, there was no escaping the reality that in leaving Ethiopia, he was not only abandoning the call to ministry—he was abandoning our family. I prayed that this time, he would change his mind and come back. This seem to be confirmed when a prophet who didn't know me at all said that three years ago I had been through something painful, and that I was worried that the same thing would happen again. "This time," he assured me, "it will be different." I hoped he meant it would be better.

After being by myself again for four months, I found myself driving around Addis Ababa, asking God, "Show me what I'm not seeing. If it's in me, then bring it to the surface and cleanse me of it so that we can move on." What transpired over the next few days was an opening of my eyes to what had become a perpetual cycle of addiction. An event had taken place across the Tasman Sea from our home country that exposed that the drinking had indeed again regained its place. I finally saw the lies, the drinking, and the deceit. When God sees something suffocating our ability to grow, in His kindness, He can and will prune it. But first, it must be exposed. God is light, and in the words of John 1:5 (ESV), "the light shines in the darkness, and the darkness has not overcome it." The image that I had fought to uphold was now about to make way for our reality to be exposed and finally cut off.

* * *

I once heard a story told of two farmers who both owned a field full of cattle. One farmer kept his cattle by fencing them in all around while the other farmer kept his cattle by keeping a well of water in the middle of the field where they dwelt with no fence at all. The latter image is a picture of the love that is our water well drawing us into the garden and close to the Gardener. *Who would want to stray from something as beautiful as pure love?*

At the end of the day, just like Adam and Eve, we all have freedom of choice. We can choose to go to the well that never runs dry or we can wander out into the wild and search for our own sources of nourishment. Addiction is like that, a searching for a fulfilment that draws you away from what can sustain you. It causes you to overlook what you have in front of you. In fact, Ed Welch, in his book, *Addictions: A Banquet in the Grave,* says, "An addiction is a worship disorder."

Addiction is much more complicated than I could have imagined when I entered into a relationship where addiction drove the majority of our behaviours. When we excuse another person's habits, and allow the blame to fall on us for what they do, we are, in essence, enabling the addiction. That is the definition of being co-dependant. Yet, when you live with that kind of manipulation and lack the boundaries necessary to distinguish what you are responsible for, you believe that you really *are* to blame for their behaviour.

While I would never have said that my husband was addicted after our original conversion of faith, I lacked an educated understanding of what that all entailed. What I came to realise was that addiction was not only about a substance or the frequency of consumption, but also about a mindset that leads to a set of behaviours that cause abuse.

My husband's abuse and anger could have been influenced by numerous things, including his culture of origin, but I often blamed myself for it. I carried the shame of it all by covering up for what I knew should have been conquered by the power of the Holy Spirit in his life. Amidst all the confusion and the blame, I had to seek God's Word and His wisdom when making the final decision as to whether to end my marriage. When I looked at all the variables around my husband's drinking and behaviour, I realised that it wasn't only at the times where I had supposedly inflicted pain on him. Abuse causes confusion and makes you feel condemned for stuff you weren't responsible for.

If God's intent was that we live without shame and condemnation, then we know that when we live under shame, we aren't experiencing the fullness of all God has for us. In that original intent, there was no shame and no confusion. In the garden, "Adam and his wife were both naked, and they felt no shame" (Genesis 2:25).

God desires the glory we fell short of to be restored back to us. He will take whatever measures necessary for us to experience that restoration. Places of insecurity can be displaced when we find security in Him, but that often means false security defaults must be dismantled. This is the process of pruning. When God talks about pruning, He is aware that it may be the very person or thing that is leading your family, your business, or your community that is actually inhibiting the growth of all those who sit beneath them. He wants *everything* to flourish and He is willing to inflict the pain of separation—of pruning—so that the *whole* tree is fruitful. When we're in the midst of this process, we must look to His Word for relief and comfort, remembering that the pain of pruning is only temporary.

> *For our light and momentary troubles are achieving for us an eternal glory that far outweighs them all. So we fix our*

> *eyes not on what is seen, but on what is unseen, since what is seen is temporary, but what is unseen is eternal.*
>
> 2 Corinthians 4:17-18

The pain we experience in the pruning is a pain that's worth embracing. When we know we are being pruned by a loving Father who has our best interests at heart, we can trust that He knows what He is doing. He is planning to restore all that we have lost in our relationships—whether that is trust, companionship, provision, kindness, love or belonging. He always plans to grow something better out of the places He prunes. Jeremiah 29:5 gives us a picture of "building houses and settling down, of planting gardens and eating what they produce." God doesn't want second best for us—He wants top quality produce. It's just a matter of time.

> *The Lord will surely comfort Zion and will look with compassion on all her ruins; he will make her deserts like Eden, her wastelands like the garden of the Lord. Joy and gladness will be found in her, thanksgiving and the sound of singing.*
>
> Isaiah 51:3

 YOUR INVITATION INTO THE GARDEN

When: *did you feel the pain of pruning in your life and what were the results?*

Where: *do you need to allow God to grow you into all He created you to be?*

What: *is your story and what are you doing so that others may learn from its glory?*

CHAPTER TEN

The Fruit

Restoring Prosperity

The final house that we rented together as a family in Debre Zeit, was a single level brick home with a huge front yard. Across the strip that ran parallel to our front veranda were three papaya trees that produced fruit constantly. Behind the papaya trees was a row of mango trees, an apple tree and two avocado trees that hung over our front fence. Mixed with the ripe bananas we could buy from the street stores, and some locally made yoghurt that was produced by the Dutch dairy business in town, we could make the most delicious smoothies to cool us down on a scorching Ethiopian afternoon.

When I walk through nature, whether by the water or in the forest, I marvel at the wonder of our God who created it all for us to enjoy. As a chef and a foodie, I love to indulge in the fruit that nature produces. Aesthetically, the intricate design in each fruit, vegetable, seed and grain, never ceases to amaze me and my pallet and stomach take pleasure in the flavours that are locked up in wholefoods.

After the Fall, even the dirt itself was no longer able to produce what God had intended it to from the beginning. But as God restores us to the garden, we find ourselves in a place where the ground we work is rich and nourished—we are positioned to bear good fruit, not only for our own enjoyment, but for the blessing of others.

HIS VESSELS

We entered into Ethiopia at the end of the rainy season and we acquainted ourselves with the struggles of hand-washing muddy clothes and the importance of keeping feet clean and covered, preventing the risk of Elephantiasis. My children ran down a road I had dreamed about four or five years earlier. We walked around our small town and kept the by-standers curious. Our faces looked similar to those who surrounded us, yet, we had slight differences.

Working with children who came from homes that struggled to provide one meal a day, kept us humble. We not only taught in their school, but we also extended our activities to visiting their homes along with short-term visitors who came to spend time with the same organisation. Their homes that were often nothing more than four walls made from sticks and mud, furnished with a mattress shared by more than one, and the stark reality of our privilege hit hard as we grappled with the enormity of their issues. As we partnered alongside fellow-westerners, we saw prayers being answered for families who had no hope of provision in any other way. Our own family got to be one such answer.

Within the first two months, one of these short-term visitors shared his burden for a boy he sponsored. The boy's mother had just given birth to twin girls while living in a small tin house in the slums and was then abandoned by her husband. With no income or support from the organisation that supported her son, she cried out to God for help. When we heard that she was about to be evicted from her home, I offered a space in our house for her small family. I knew what it was like to have twins and then have their father disappoint you straight after. I'd had the privilege of being in a western country where the government stepped in and provided an income for us, but she didn't. However, we were part of a different government that sat upon the shoulders of King Jesus—the kingdom of God. As part of that government, I believed we had a responsibility to steward our blessings and represent our King well.

The four of them came and shifted into our bedroom while we slept Samoan-style, on the floor of our living room for six weeks. The mother shared a dream where Jesus brought her what she needed to look after her babies, thanking us for being the vessels God chose for His providence. I was overwhelmed that He was using us to make dreams come true for women like her. They became a part of our family, teaching us some Amharic language as we tried to navigate through daily expectations and communicate through translators who were barely present. After six weeks, she moved out and found sponsors to take on the living expenses she needed for her family. As she left, she asked me, "How long will you stay in Ethiopia?" I told her I wanted to see her twin girls graduate high school before I left.

Although there were huge challenges with power, water, phone and internet coverage, our life was an adventure lived out to enrich the lives of others and build capacity within our own. This is the kind of life God wants for all His children. He wants us to be a source of blessing and provision for the world. He wants to,

> *. . . open the heavens, the storehouse of his bounty, to send rain on your land in season and to bless all the work of your hands. You will lend to many nations but will borrow from none. The Lord will make you the head, not the tail. If you pay attention to the commands of the Lord your God that I give you this day and carefully follow them, you will always be at the top, never at the bottom.*
>
> Deuteronomy 28:12-13

In Isaiah 61, when God lists the areas in which He wants to restore us in our holistic make up, He mentions finances first because nothing competes for our attention and affection more than money. From time to time, we need to take inventory of our finances and see where they fit in the great landscape of our life. *Has money occupied too much space in our mind or in our heart? Or does worrying about it consume us instead?* In Matthew 6, we read a lesson Jesus gave to His disciples about their finances. After talking about giving to the poor and the importance of praying and fasting, He reminds them:

> *No one can serve two masters. Either you will hate the one and love the other, or you will be devoted to the one and despise the other. You cannot serve both God and money.*
>
> Matthew 6:24

Money can so easily become the idol that takes up the space that only God should enthrone in our lives. When it becomes our love, our drive, our world, then it leads to all kinds of evil. Fortunately, Jesus has given us the antidote for this evil:

> *So do not worry, saying, 'What shall we eat?' or 'What shall we drink?' or 'What shall we wear?' For the pagans run after all these things, and your*

> *heavenly Father knows that you need them. But seek first his kingdom and his righteousness, and all these things will be given to you as well.*
>
> Matthew 6:31-33

Jesus is drawing attention to the fact that, ultimately our drive to earn more money and store it up is connected to our fear of not having enough to meet our basic needs for survival. He reminds us if we take care of His kingdom, He will take care of us. His kingdom is far more than the institution of 'church'; it is the entirety of the work He is doing across the earth. When we partner with Him financially, we partner with Him in this work. I love the example of generosity Paul shares with us in 2 Corinthians 9:6-15. Look at the holistic effect and impact of this one church's gift:

> *Whoever sows sparingly will also reap sparingly, and whoever sows generously will also reap generously. Each of you should give what you have decided in your heart to give, not reluctantly or under compulsion, for God loves a cheerful giver. And God is able to bless you abundantly, so that in all things at all times, having all that you need, you will abound in every good work. As it is written: 'They have freely scattered their gifts to the poor; their righteousness endures forever.' Now he who supplies seed to the sower and bread for food will also supply and increase your store of seed and will enlarge the harvest of your righteousness. You will be enriched in every way so that you can be generous on every occasion, and through us your generosity will result in thanksgiving to God.*
>
> *This service that you perform is not only supplying the needs of the Lord's people but is also overflowing in many expressions of thanks to God. Because of the service by which you have proved yourselves, others will praise God for the obedience that accompanies your confession of the gospel of Christ, and for your*

generosity in sharing with them and with everyone else. And in their prayers for you their hearts will go out to you, because of the surpassing grace God has given you. Thanks be to God for his indescribable gift!

As our lives become fruitful, our capacity to bless others increases. What we need to bring to this stage of our lives is a generous spirit. Generosity does not only restore us financially; it restores us holistically. There is a flow-on effect to our mental wellbeing as endorphins are released when we give, making us feel good after being generous and offering our services. In fact, multiple streams are restored so that we can "be generous on every occasion" (2 Corinthians 9:11). The gift or service the Corinthian believers performed was a spiritual act of thanksgiving because they were sharing what they could have kept to themselves. The recipients of this gift were the church in Macedonia who would be restored socially, knowing that they were being looked after by others. Paul commended the Corinthians in the previous chapter by saying something that is important for us to understand:

> *Our desire is not that others might be relieved while you are hard pressed, but that there might be equality. At the present time your plenty will supply what they need, so that in turn their plenty will supply what you need. The goal is equality, as it is written: 'The one who gathered much did not have too much, and the one who gathered little did not have too little.'*
>
> 2 Corinthians 8:13-15

Yes, God has great things in store for your finances. He doesn't want you to live in poverty, or for others to take advantage of your hard-earned money. We are responsible for the place in which money has power in our lives. If you think that you will run out if you give, this mentality needs to be broken. God's plans for us are to prosper us, so we have to trust that His commands are going to work for our good.

As we listen to the promptings of the Holy Spirit, and give lavishly to those in need, we reflect the heart of God Himself. God will never ask us to do what He hasn't already been willing to do Himself! He is generous in every way toward us. The scriptures tell us that though Jesus was rich, yet for our sake He became poor, so that we "through his poverty might become rich" (2 Corinthians 8:9). Likewise, in 2 Peter 1:3 (NLT) we read that in His divine power, God gives us "everything we need for living a godly life."

* * *

Being content with what we have is one of the keys to stewarding our fruitfulness well. Adam and Eve found this out in the original garden:

> But the Lord God warned him, 'You may *freely* eat the fruit of every tree in the garden, except the tree of the knowledge of good and evil. If you eat its fruit, you are sure to die.'
>
> Genesis 2:16-17, NLT

Every tree except one was given to Adam and Eve in the garden, yet the enemy subtly deceived them into thinking that the one tree they were forbidden to eat from, was the one they really needed. The insurmountable debt that is upon the world today is because of lack of contentment with what we have. May we remember what God has given us and be satisfied with that. When our lives are blessed with fruitfulness in every area, there will be plenty left to give. As we enrich the lives of individuals and communities with our generosity, we find that we are in fact, partnering with God for the transformation of the world!

🌿 YOUR INVITATION INTO THE GARDEN

When: *do you plan to set up a financial plan that includes a budget for giving?*

Where: *does your income come from? Do you have multiple streams so that you can survive if your main stream gets cut off?*

What: *can you do this week to activate a change that you know needs to happen?*

CHAPTER ELEVEN

The Boundaries

Restoring Freedom

As you drive through the gates of Desta Mender, you'll travel down a long gravel road that is lined with Eucalyptus trees. To the left is a small man-made lake that sits below a café which was built to teach women culinary skills. Behind the café is a hill lined with seasonal vegetables grown using modern day hydroponic systems. Then a large field of green grass stretches out into a housing village, backed by a hospital training school and dormitories for the students. Desta Menda means 'Joy Village' in English and was named by Dr Catherine Hamlin, the Australian woman who began the Fistula hospital in Addis Ababa. She decided to set up this beautiful space for the women who had gone beyond the point of no return by the damage that had been done to their bodies. Lack of physical repair for them meant social isolation in their family of origin, so they found new freedom and joy within the safety of this village.

> *So I have come down to rescue them from the hand of the Egyptians and to bring them up out of that land into a good and spacious land, a land flowing with milk and honey.*
>
> Exodus 3:8

THE GARDEN GRANTS US FREEDOM. EGYPT, IN the context of this verse, represented slavery and oppression, and God desires to set us free from slavery of any sort. Jesus came so that we might be free—even from the law that governed the people of Israel as a result of their Exodus and lack of structure and boundaries.

The Garden of Eden was a spacious place, a place without limitations or constrictions, a place of peace and prosperity. It's no wonder that our hearts yearn for what we were created for, and as a result desire peace on Earth. It's not surprising that our hearts are broken for the poor, the sick and the injustices we see around us when we understand that this was never meant to be our reality.

I believe that when righteous indignation rises in our hearts, it is God awakening us to align with His heart for the restoration of humanity. Ecclesiastes 3:11 says that God has "set eternity in the human heart" and so we have this navigation system—a True North that points our hearts and conscience to a way that is greater than ourselves.

Eternity is ultimately where full restoration will occur. It exists outside the scope of time and in an unseen realm; it's a place we call Heaven. The apostle John, while on the island of Patmos, not far from my grandparent's Greek birthplace, wrote about it. The book of Revelation describes the restoration of Eden as he saw it in this vision:

> *Then the angel showed me the river of the water of life, as clear as crystal, flowing from the throne of God and of the Lamb down the middle of the great street of the city. On each side of the river stood the tree of life, bearing*

> *twelve crops of fruit, yielding its fruit every month. And the leaves of the tree are for the healing of the nations.*
>
> Revelation 22:1-2

Eden has been restored. Even though we cannot see it yet, one day we will. It is there waiting for us to leave this life and enter into an eternal dwelling place where all that was taken away will be restored. It is there that God "will wipe every tear from [our] eyes. There will be no more death or mourning or crying or pain, for the old order of things has passed away." (Revelation 21:4)

But how does that help us in our suffering today? Yes it can give us hope for beyond this life, but you may be asking how this applies to your current situation. I know that in the trials of my life, when the end is too far out of reach, the only solution I have seen as an escape has been to determine my own end by taking my own life. This is not unlike even some of the prophets in the Bible. Yet this advice that Paul gives the church in Corinth, has come as a means of adjusting my perspective in these hard places:

> *Therefore we do not lose heart. Though outwardly we are wasting away, yet inwardly we are being renewed day by day. For our light and momentary troubles are achieving for us an eternal glory that far outweighs them all. So we fix our eyes not on what is seen, but on what is unseen, since what is seen is temporary, but what is unseen is eternal.*
>
> 2 Corinthians 4:16-18

We are holistic beings. Though one part may feel like its wasting away, another part is being strengthened. This is the benefit of having multiple streams that are flowing down banks that grant us freedom to keep hope alive. When I have been tempted to let the "momentary troubles" get me down, I pray. In a moment of prayer I can be transported from the problems of this world into an eternal reality that is magnified by the fact that I am praying to a God who is greater than my problems.

When we know Jesus as a friend, He invites us to come to Him with our burdens and find rest. He wants us to rest from judging others, but all too often we find ourselves back in that place. It is far too easy to lose heart when our eyes are fixed on others—judging them by their weaknesses or comparing ourselves to their strengths. Jesus came to give us a life in abundance! He doesn't want us to take on the responsibility of other's actions, so we need to take responsibility for ourselves. As we do, we find freedom and we find our identity in who He has created us to be.

> *Therefore, if anyone is in Christ, the new creation has come: The old has gone, the new is here! All this is from God, who reconciled us to himself through Christ and gave us the ministry of reconciliation: that God was reconciling the world to Himself in Christ, not counting people's sins against them. And He has committed to us the message of reconciliation. We are therefore Christ's ambassadors, as though God were making his appeal through us. We implore you on Christ's behalf: Be reconciled to God. God made Him who had no sin to be sin for us, so that in him we might become the righteousness of God.*
>
> 2 Corinthians 5:17-21

This whole passage is mind-blowing to me. It articulates God's desire to make right what Adam made wrong, *and* what we made wrong! He gives us a clean slate by sending Jesus to pay for our sin Himself. He reconciles us, bringing again into unity, harmony and agreement what was alienated in the original sin that took place in the garden of Eden. It says that God was in Christ and that when we are "in Christ" we can join Him there.

In the spirit realm, we are given an opportunity to be 'born again.' The term in the original Greek text is *gennaō* (born) meaning "to regenerate" and *aṅōthen* (again) meaning "from above, anew." We are regenerated from above and seen by God as we were originally intended to be created. "God was *in* Christ reconciling the world to Himself", giving us an opportunity to be the first of many and He had it all planned out before we were even born.

> *For those God foreknew He also predestined to be conformed to the image of his Son, that He might be the firstborn among many brothers and sisters.*
>
> Romans 8:29

> *And we all, who with unveiled faces contemplate the Lord's glory, are being transformed into his image with ever-increasing glory, which comes from the Lord, who is the Spirit.*
>
> 2 Corinthians 3:18

There is a ripple effect of this reunion with God in the spirit realm. It is not only for our benefit but it is for the benefit of others as we then become His ambassadors. Maybe we don't feel like we can represent Him well or that we are inadequate to do that job, but the more we represent Him, the more like Him we become. And what did He come to do? To seek and to save those who are lost and to love them back to Him. As we do this, the mourning we feel for what was lost and what can no longer be, is replaced with joy.

> *To all who mourn in Israel, he will give a crown of beauty for ashes, a joyous blessing instead of mourning, festive praise instead of despair.*
>
> Isaiah 61:3, NLT

Becoming the best version of you is about aligning yourself with the person God originally intended you to be, the you of the Garden. It is when we can draw down from Heaven all that we need to represent Him well on this Earth, and look back to Heaven when our eyes are tempted to look down, that festive praise replaces despair.

> *The Lord will guide you always; He will satisfy your needs in a sun-scorched land and will strengthen your frame. You will be like a well-watered garden, like a spring whose waters never fail.*
>
> Isaiah 58:11

You are intended to be a well-watered garden. The water that wells up within your garden experience, flows out to others and waters them. This life isn't just about you. It is also about others; it's about championing a cause that's greater than yourself and helping to meet needs where possible. Remember that Love is the soil that you need to draw from. Love well, trust God and keep your eyes fixed on Him and your garden will never run dry.

We are on this journey called "Life". Even though our hearts long for this land of milk and honey, we will never fully get there until we enter into eternity. It is as if we are in the courtyard of a garden—travelling through the wilderness before we enter the Promised Land. We are in a garden space but not the Garden itself. So, we have to encourage each other when we go through different seasons that exist around the garden space we are in right now. Ecclesiastes 3:1-8 says that there is a time for everything:

> *A time to be born and a time to die,*
> *a time to plant and a time to uproot,*
> *a time to kill and a time to heal,*
> *a time to tear down and a time to build,*
> *a time to weep and a time to laugh,*

a time to mourn and a time to dance,
a time to scatter stones and a time to gather them,
a time to embrace and a time to refrain from embracing,
a time to search and a time to give up,
a time to keep and a time to throw away,
a time to tear and a time to mend,
a time to be silent and a time to speak,
a time to love and a time to hate,
a time for war and a time for peace.

May God help us to be patient in every season and to discern His timing in everything. I know that this was the right time for me to write this book, so I pray that whoever reads it will be touched by His Spirit and connect not just to my story but to His redemption in all of it. God is the Greatest Gardener, the Kindest Father, the Kinsman Redeemer who has paid for us to be reconciled with Himself. We can hold onto the hope that one day, we will again see Eden restored.

 YOUR INVITATION INTO THE GARDEN

Where: *do you feel eternity rise in your heart the most?*

What: *do you need to let go of, in order to receive true freedom?*

When: *did you open your heart to Jesus and let Him restore you eternally?*

CHAPTER TWELVE

The Future

Restoring Hope

Oceans roar around the vast border of Australia, the birthplace of my father and the new home of my family. Blue waves beat up against the beautiful red rocks that sit beneath the white tombstones of the Waverley Cemetery. Sitting between Clovelly and Bronte beaches, this stretch of the coastal walk on Sydney's Eastern Beaches never fails to demand a pause. As we walk along the bridge that sits in between, we are reminded of the contrast between death and life, potential gone unrealised, buried in the ground, and potential still available if we would dare possess it. Grief and joy, walking side by side. Hope that yet another day dawns with each sunrise, and with each new day, an opportunity to live again.

"Y̲OU ARE GLOWING," EXCLAIMED MY COUSIN WHO had not seen me in two years. Even she could see that there was something different about my appearance and my countenance. What she wasn't aware of, was that this "glow" came with the confidence that I now know to be true, what I had held onto by faith for so many years.

When I landed in Sydney in late September 2016, my plan was to stay for three months. Knowing there was a better day coming, I went on a journey of holistic restoration. I was intentionally building capacity for what God had said He would do while I was in the midst of my despair. Words of hope came in the form of a whisper that He would "send someone to show me true love." Scriptures stood out to me that reminded me that there would be a restoration of what I had lost relationally—a marriage, a wedding, a union that would exemplify God's heart for His people. Intentional as I was, however, I could never have coordinated the people, the timing and the methods by which my restoration would come.

Finding myself at thirty-eight years of age living with my mum in Sydney, Australia, with four of my five children, was never my plan. But God was placing me in the perfect location. Little did I know that we would end up living seven minutes from Hillsong Church which would play a major role in my restorative journey.

One thing I quickly realised was that my identity had been placed around certain positions I had held: a wife, a missionary, a minister of the Word, a mother. In Australia I was completely anonymous. Nobody knew my background or my qualifications. I was just another face in the crowd and I had to become content with that. Placing reminders on the bathroom mirror of who I was in God's eyes, wasn't just a trendy thing to do—it was a pivotal exercise to rewire the way I thought about myself:

"You are chosen, You are accepted, You are loved by Love Himself."

"You are beautiful, You are valuable, You are created for such a time as this."

Over time I had to rethink my plans to return to Ethiopia. "Sometimes God calls us to go, and sometimes He calls us to stay," someone told me. Those were hard words to swallow, and I cried at the thought of being stuck in Australia. In hindsight though, I can see that God was restoring me back to the land from which my father had fled in his early adulthood.

When I accepted the challenge to stay in Australia, I wanted to be in an environment where I could hear from God. I enrolled in Hillsong College and took the one subject that really interested me at the time: Mission and Culture. Like a good debriefing session after an event, this class allowed me to process the cross-cultural experience I had just returned from. And, it allowed me to see my current place of residence as a new mission field that God was calling me to. Little did I know that it would be a long-term mission.

During my first year back in Australia, I often questioned God. The heat of the first summer was almost unbearable and we were living in a two-bedroom apartment with no air conditioning. When my children would ask why we lived there I would remind them that we were there "for a season and for a reason." Yet I too failed to make sense of it all on days that felt like there was a furnace burning under our house. On the bed I shared with my mother (who was suffering from sleep apnea), I cried out to God and heard Him speak to me in three ways—through a vision, a dream, and a scripture.

In my vision, I was in the front carpark of our church building. There, a large golden chiffon cloth was placed over me like a dome. I was dancing around underneath the safety it provided, and then I saw God's hand pick it up and stretch it out. When I woke out of the vision, my immediate interpretation was that God was extending the scope of my dwelling place, just as He says in Isaiah 54:2-6:

Enlarge the place of your tent,
stretch your tent curtains wide, do not hold back;

> lengthen your cords, strengthen your stakes.
> For you will spread out to the right and to the left;
> your descendants will dispossess nations
> and settle in their desolate cities.
> Do not be afraid; you will not be put to shame.
> Do not fear disgrace; you will not be humiliated.
> You will forget the shame of your youth
> and remember no more
> the reproach of your widowhood.
> For your Maker is your husband—
> the Lord Almighty is his name—
> the Holy One of Israel is your Redeemer;
> he is called the God of all the earth.
> The Lord will call you back
> as if you were a wife deserted
> and distressed in spirit—
> a wife who married young,
> only to be rejected," says your God.

The dream I had was actually two consecutive dreams with a word in the middle. The first was an image of pieces of my past—parts I had blocked from my memory and didn't want to see. In the second, I was riding on a bike with my youngest son when a man came from behind me and held me in his arms so sweetly, like I had never felt before. In the middle of those two dreams a word kept repeating in my mind—Juxtaposition. When I looked up the meaning of that word, I read, "the fact of two things being seen or placed close together with contrasting effect." God was reminding me that my past was going to look so much different than my future; that what lay ahead was bright and full of a beauty I had never experienced before.

The third way God spoke to me was through His Word. Opening up my Bible one day in the middle of a heat wave, I found myself reading the story of Jesus' crucifixion.

> *Near the cross of Jesus stood his mother, his mother's sister, Mary the wife of Clopas, and Mary Magdalene. When Jesus saw his mother there, and the disciple whom he loved standing nearby, he said to her, 'Woman, here is your son,' and to the disciple, 'Here is your mother.' From that time on, this disciple took her into his home.*
>
> John 19:25-27

Desipte his struggles, my father often opened up his Bible to a certain spot and recited what he had read—and in this moment, I was emulating his example. Desperate for a solution to my problem of being alone, I said to God, "I want it to be like this. When you bring my husband into my life, I want you to say to him, 'here is your wife,' and to me, 'here is your husband.'" I wasn't about to go searching for a man who would show me true love; I was staking my claim on what God had previously promised.

One month later, I filled out the form to apply for bible college, and shortly after, the pastoral leader who read my application called to find out a bit more of my story. As a result, she referred me to the pastoral counsellor on the church staff who dealt specifically with women who had been in domestically violent relationships. It wasn't until I was able to name this, that I was able to find healing for it. She then referred me to a qualified counsellor who nurtured my mind and brain back to wholeness. It was a two-year intensive journey that took this broken, divorcee to a confident single woman.

Soon, I began to understand why God had brought me back to Australia. Within a short distance of my home were so many services and programs—from Alcoholics Anonymous, to community support groups, to a program called, "Shine" which I originally thought was for teenage girls and sent my daughters along till I found out that I could join in too! All around me, as I shared my story, I found others who resonated with the struggles I had faced—women who had been in relationships with addicts, abusers, and narcissists. As I was finding my healing, God was using me to help bring healing to others.

I was making progress in so many areas of life. I had found work to support my kids, built a community of friends around me, started a business and run a half marathon just before I turned forty. Yet I sensed there was still something missing.

* * *

On the afternoon just before I was due to fly back to Ethiopia to sign my exit visa and pack up our belongings to settle in Australia, I sat in the café at church across from a young man. He was a student from Singapore and was reading a book about relationships. Having heard of this book, I started up a conversation about its contents. Not only did this young man share the theme behind the book but also some of his convictions regarding relationships and purity. He proceeded to tell me of some advice he had given to married couples and perhaps as he had seen my facial expressions change, explained himself. "I don't give advice out of life experience, but out of revelation that the Holy Spirit is telling me." He was only in his early twenties, and I was curious about this gift he claimed to have and tested it, asking if he had any "words of knowledge" for me.

"Yes, I do," he replied. "But I didn't know you so I didn't want to say anything." After I had given him permission to go ahead, he proceeded to tell me what I already knew. He said that he had seen a picture of me in a cold bed and it made him want to cry. He said that there had been generational problems with relationships in my family line and that God was calling me to break the curse. At first, I started to shrink back, thinking that he was going to be another one to advise that I "fight for my marriage", but actually, he was calling me to fight for the generations to come. With a smile on his face he said, "but there is good news. I also saw that you are going to be in a warm bed and that you are going to show your children what a healthy relationship looks like. As a result, they too will have healthy relationships—so get ready!"

Oh, I thought, I was already ready! I even thought I knew who God had in mind. But here I am, four years later convinced that God knows so much better than I do. In February 2020, as the world was about to change as a result of a pandemic, I was applying for a job. It had been a year of unemployment, trying to work a business and grow a network, a year where God was reminding me to rest and praise Him, a year that had me on my knees and in classes that reminded me of the vision He had given me. Now, I was about to see the salvation of the Lord.

Lamentations 3:19-27 says:

> *I remember my affliction and my wandering,*
> *the bitterness and the gall.*
> *I well remember them,*
> *and my soul is downcast within me.*
> *Yet this I call to mind*
> *and therefore I have hope:*
> *Because of the Lord's great love we are not consumed,*
> *for his compassions never fail.*
> *They are new every morning;*
> *great is your faithfulness.*
> *I say to myself, "The Lord is my portion;*
> *therefore I will wait for him."*
> *The Lord is good to those whose hope is in him,*
> *to the one who seeks him;*
> *it is good to wait quietly*
> *for the salvation of the Lord.*
> *It is good for a man to bear the yoke while he is young.*

Hope. That was what a young man in Canada had reminded me to hold onto at the beginning of 2020. He had sent me a private message on Instagram the day after I went on a date for the second time since being 'single'. It read, "I feel from the Lord that you are waiting on someone. Keep waiting. Don't lose hope. You will reap if you do not lose hope. You're amazing! Be blessed this year. Don't waiver on the promise, don't quit. Don't look in another direction. Just be confident in who you are and what God has spoken. You are where you are supposed to be."

The author of this message was a young man who had visited Ethiopia at significant times in my marriage journey—both times my children and I had been abandoned by my husband. He had seen me at my worst and, like an angel, had come to support my family. Now his message injected hope into me about the promises that God had given me—promises I hadn't uttered to many, as the prospect of them coming true seemed too good to be true, perhaps yet another fantasy or illusion I had conjured up in my mind.

* * *

I had just completed the job interview that sealed my position as a relationships coordinator with Mission Aviation Fellowship. The position fit perfectly into my life experience, my heart's desires, and my strengths that I had just learned about the year before. It was one way that God restored my calling and vocation. Now, here I am sixteen months later, working from an office just five minutes from my home, having prayed thousands of prayers over hundreds of church leaders, for an income that is beyond what I ever imagined. It has been a space where I have been able to grow as I am nurtured by a healthy leadership team. It has also been a space where I have been able to share in a 'ministry of acquaintance' as I have got to know people who are not only on the mission field but those who have previously spent time as overseas missionaries.

That night after my interview, I wrote in my journal that I keep seeing the number 444. These were the first three digits of our phone number growing up in Glenfield, New Zealand, and here I was in my new home in Glenwood, Australia. I noted that it was also coming up to the fourth anniversary of the flight that would separate me from the one I had taken my vows with. I also realised that it spoke of 'ministry', forty-four months being approximately the length of time Jesus spent doing ministry on earth.

Four months later, I found myself at the house of a man who had started a Facebook prayer platform with his brother after he had lost his wife of thirty years. I had been referred to this online group when I was desperate for people to pray with me while churches were closed and social restrictions were tightly enforced due to the pandemic. The people who were sharing live videos and praying every day on this public platform, had become like family to me, so meeting them in person was exciting and nerve-wracking at the same time.

As Marcus opened the door to greet me, he stood tall against a couple of the other guys who stood near him. We walked into the house together and sat in front of his computer where we were about to go live on this cold Saturday night. As usual, we entered into worship together as I had done so many times from my home. I had no idea who these people were, or what their backgrounds were like, but I felt safe in their company. When it came time to speak, Marcus unexpectedly handed me the phone and asked me to introduce myself. Little did I know that I was to be a guest speaker that night! It had been years since I had had a preaching opportunity. In fact, my pastor's wife in Ethiopia would regularly ask me, "Michelle, are you preaching yet?" and I would mourn for the days when I did. Yet the message God had laid on my heart that night was the promise He had placed in my spirit:

> *To all who mourn in Israel, he will give a crown of beauty for ashes, a joyous blessing instead of mourning, festive praise instead of despair.*
>
> Isaiah 61:3 NLT

After the livestream, we shared a meal and our hearts. Before I left that night, the hosts packed up some leftovers for me to take home to my children who were waiting for me. Over time, these people became my friends and this platform has become my pulpit. We all began walking together along the shore lines of Sydney, exploring parts of our beautiful city without the crowds that tourism would normally bring.

As one month turned into another and another, I could see how God, the whole time, had not only prepared my life for Ethiopia, but also for my ministry, work and life in Australia. Nothing was wasted, all was preparation and perhaps, God was preparing me for His promise.

To be continued . . .

Recommended Resources

Multiple streams of resources are my recommendation, but here are a few that have helped me in my journey of holistic restoration:

Psychological—Restoring the Heart
Dan Allender |www.theallendercenter.org

Social—Restoring Relationships
Dr Henry Cloud |www.boundaries.me

Financial—Restoration from Debt
Dave Ramsay |www.ramseysolutions.com

Physical—Restoring the Body
Dr Don Colbert |www.drcolbert.com
Prekure |www.prekure.com

Vocational—Restoring Purpose
Clifton Strengths |www.gallup.com

Spiritual—Restoring the Spirit
Peter Scazzero |www.emotionallyhealthy.org
Priscilla Shirer |Breathe: Making Room for Sabbath

Acknowledgements

I wish to acknowledge a handful of people:

The team at Torn Curtain Publishing
for helping me to get this book out there.

My friend, Stella Muller
who supported me in my mission to Ethiopia and in publishing this book.

My mum, Iva Zombos
for the countless times she babysat my children while I went away for some writing time.

My counsellor, Vanessa Ong
who has been my navigator in this journey of holistic restoration.

My siblings, Anita, Tanya, Kathy and Constantine
and their families, for being my greatest support team—I couldn't have asked for better people to do this life with.

and last but not least,

My children, Jamal, Kiara, Lydia, Matthias and Wesley
for wandering with me through the wilderness and for allowing me to share our story.

www.ingramcontent.com/pod-product-compliance
Lightning Source LLC
Chambersburg PA
CBHW030258010526
44107CB00053B/1751